Innovation Policies for Inclusive Growth

This work is published under the responsibility of the Secretary-General of the OECD. The opinions expressed and arguments employed herein do not necessarily reflect the official views of OECD member countries.

This document and any map included herein are without prejudice to the status of or sovereignty over any territory, to the delimitation of international frontiers and boundaries and to the name of any territory, city or area.

Please cite this publication as:
OECD (2015), *Innovation Policies for Inclusive Growth*, OECD Publishing, Paris.
http://dx.doi.org/10.1787/9789264229488-en

ISBN 978-92-64-22941-9 (print)
ISBN 978-92-64-22948-8 (PDF)

The statistical data for Israel are supplied by and under the responsibility of the relevant Israeli authorities. The use of such data by the OECD is without prejudice to the status of the Golan Heights, East Jerusalem and Israeli settlements in the West Bank under the terms of international law.

Photo credits: © Storm – Fotolia.com; © iStockphoto.com/il67.

Corrigenda to OECD publications may be found on line at: *www.oecd.org/publishing/corrigenda.htm*.
© OECD 2015

You can copy, download or print OECD content for your own use, and you can include excerpts from OECD publications, databases and multimedia products in your own documents, presentations, blogs, websites and teaching materials, provided that suitable acknowledgement of OECD as source and copyright owner is given. All requests for public or commercial use and translation rights should be submitted to *rights@oecd.org*. Requests for permission to photocopy portions of this material for public or commercial use shall be addressed directly to the Copyright Clearance Center (CCC) at *info@copyright.com* or the Centre français d'exploitation du droit de copie (CFC) at *contact@cfcopies.com*.

Table of contents

Executive summary 5

Chapter 1. **Scaling up inclusive innovations** 9
    1. The context of inclusive innovation 10
    2. In what ways are inclusive innovations different? 16
    3. What is the impact of inclusive innovations? 24
    4. Conclusion 30
    Notes 31
    References 31

Chapter 2. **Inclusive innovations in education** 35
    1. Characteristics of inclusive innovations in education 36
    2. Scaling up 40
    3. Conclusion 45
    Notes 45
    References 45

Chapter 3. **Policies in support of inclusive innovation** 47
    1. The role of innovation policies in supporting inclusive innovation 48
    2. Co-operation challenges 51
    3. Policy instruments supporting inclusive innovation 56
    4. Conclusion 62
    Notes 63
    References 63

Chapter 4. **The search for excellence and the democratisation of innovation** 67
    1. Inclusive growth and innovation 68
    2. Industrial inclusiveness 71
    3. The democratisation of innovation 79
    4. Trickle-down dynamics: Diffusion and its impacts on industrial inclusiveness ... 84
    5. The impacts of innovation policies on inclusiveness 90
    6. Open questions on the economics of innovation and inclusive growth 93
    7. Conclusion 94
    Notes 95
    References 95

Tables
    1.1. Examples of pro-inclusive and grassroots innovations 11
    1.2. Characteristics and examples of inclusive innovations compared with standard innovations 19

1.3. Particularities of grassroots innovations compared with standard and pro-inclusive innovations 21
1.4. Pricing and financing strategies 26
1.5. Changing production practices 27
3.1. Roadmap for successful implementation of partnerships with citizens and community organisations in public service production 55
4.1. Top 15 firms from emerging economies in the EU Industrial Investment Scoreboard 2013 72
4.2. Statistics on technology use of the informal sector 88
4.3. Economic conditions and their impacts on innovation 92

Figures

1.1. Financial inclusion of the population (2011) (% age 15+) 23
1.2. Scale of mobile health applications in Haiti, India and Kenya, 2010 (number of unique users or transactions) 25
2.1. Performance on the mathematics scale, by national deciles of the PISA index of social, economic and cultural status (2012) 39
3.1. Obstacles to inclusive innovation and types of possible policy responses 50
3.2. Actors for inclusive innovation 52
4.1. GDP growth, poverty reduction and change in Gini coefficient 70
4.2. R&D spending and income inequality after five years 71
4.3. BERD by size class of firms, 2011 73
4.4. Firms with trademarks and patents, by size, 2009-11 73
4.5. Regional distribution of innovative activity: Patents 75
4.6. National R&D expenditure concentration by top 10% TL2 regions with largest R&D expenditure as a percentage of national R&D expenditure 76
4.7. Share of co-patents by location of partners, TL3 regions, average 2008-10 79
4.8. Patenting activity of young firms by sector, 2009-11 80
4.9. Average life expectancy at birth for British elites compared with the general population, 1500-1919 85
4.10. Share of firms communicating with clients and suppliers through e-mail in 2006-11 88
4.11. Share of R&D-performing firms in liberalised versus non-liberalised industries in India 92

Follow OECD Publications on:

http://twitter.com/OECD_Pubs
http://www.facebook.com/OECDPublications
http://www.linkedin.com/groups/OECD-Publications-4645871
http://www.youtube.com/oecdilibrary
http://www.oecd.org/oecddirect/

Executive summary

Policy makers are confronted with the challenge of boosting economic growth while ensuring that gains remain socially inclusive.

Innovation is a driver of income growth and can help address poverty and directly improve well-being of different groups in society. Under certain conditions the gains from innovation benefit everybody in society; in other cases on the contrary, they might reinforce social exclusion.

Inclusive innovations' contribution to social inclusiveness

"Inclusive innovation" projects are initiatives that directly serve the welfare of lower-income and excluded groups. Inclusive innovations often modify existing technologies, products or services to better meet the needs of those groups. Examples include the Tata Nano, a low-cost car produced in India based on a no-frills strategy, and the Narayana Hrudayalaya Cardiac Care Centre which provides heart surgery at a much lower price due to business process innovations.

Inclusive innovation will only be successful if it reaches a much larger segment of poor and excluded populations than it currently does. Scaling up requires initiatives that are built around: 1) financially sustainable business models; and 2) participation by lower-income and excluded groups.

Meeting these objectives, however, is challenging. In many countries, a large segment of the population has low income levels, hindering citizens' ability to take advantage of innovation and new technologies. Companies often lack adequate knowledge on the needs of poor populations. Infrastructure is in many cases inadequate, making it costly for companies to distribute products to poorer customers.

Nevertheless, information and communication technologies (ICTs) as well as other emerging technologies offer new opportunities. The growing importance of emerging markets, including People's Republic of China (hereafter 'China') and India, also contributes by orienting business interests towards innovations that serve lower-income markets.

Inclusive innovations in education

Inclusive innovations in education can be particularly valuable, as they allow children and adults from socio-economically disadvantaged backgrounds to gain the knowledge and skills necessary to participate fully in the economy. An example is Text to Change, an innovation project that sends out text messages with information on issues such as health care, education and economic development.

Inclusive innovations in education share many of the characteristics of other inclusive innovations, but also present some specificity. Innovative educational programmes are often developed within the public education system; they may also be privately developed not-for-profit initiatives, funded mainly through public budgets or philanthropic means, or hybrid projects using for-profit models to fund not-for-profit programmes. Strong not-for-profit funding in this sector makes reaching financial sustainability less crucial in this area than in others.

Policies in support of inclusive innovations

Governments can support inclusive innovation through multiple channels. The following approaches are particularly pertinent:

- Supporting the use of advanced technologies – including those such as mobile telephony that can serve as platforms for multiple services – by steering institutional research towards the development of inclusive innovations.
  - The MIT D-Lab supports inclusive innovation from development to commercialisation by supplying technical expertise.
- Ensuring that regulatory impediments do not prohibit or constrain innovations serving the poor (particularly with regard to public services), while still ensuring critical quality standards are being met.
  - M-PESA, a mobile payment company that has become virtually ubiquitous in Kenya, has been unable to develop successfully elsewhere due to regulatory impediments.
- Addressing regulatory challenges for socially oriented entrepreneurs that seek to address the needs of low-income groups in a profit-making setting.
- Developing credit options to stabilise the income of the poor through predictable demand.
  - Microsaving and microcredit institutions render the very poor less vulnerable to income shocks.
- Developing financing mechanisms in support of inclusive innovation initiatives.
- Supporting intermediary institutions and other means of knowledge exchange to provide technical expertise to grassroots innovators and information on the needs of the poor to pro-inclusive innovators.
  - The Honey Bee Network helps grassroots innovators by providing the support needed to develop these innovators' inventions.
- Involving ministries beyond those specifically in charge of innovation, such as those focusing on rural development, education, health or infrastructure, by creating joint programmes with collaborative governance structures.
- Firmly inserting inclusive innovation policies in the innovation policy agenda, thereby ensuring policy coherence around an objective on achieving both growth and inclusiveness.

Search for excellence and democratisation of inclusive innovation

A broader question arises regarding innovation, a critical driver of growth, and its impacts on inclusiveness of such growth. Growth is critically important for emerging and developing economies and can contribute to social inclusiveness, notably by generating employment.

Innovation-led growth will also have implications for industrial and territorial inclusiveness, i.e. the extent to which the distribution of innovation capacities evolves evenly across the economy, between firms, regions, universities and public research institutes. As economies become increasingly knowledge-based, different trends with regard to industrial and territorial inclusiveness can be observed across developed, emerging and developing economies alike:

- Evidence from two knowledge outputs – patents and publications – shows that only a very small share of ideas have "high value". One of the main reasons why ideas translate into skewed value distribution relates to the nature of knowledge: marginal costs are low and, thus, successful ideas can easily capture entire markets, replacing all others. These dynamics may in turn lead to a stronger concentration of innovation capacities among actors, since agglomeration and reputation benefits reward those generating winning ideas.

- By contrast, forces supporting greater industrial inclusiveness are also at work: ICTs have opened new opportunities for small-scale entrepreneurs to become successful innovators, supporting the "democratisation of innovation", as the group of successful innovators widens to include actors that did not previously participate in innovation processes.

Industrial and territorial inclusiveness will also depend on policies that generate a favourable environment for innovation, the diffusion of innovation and other framework conditions.

Chapter 1

Scaling up inclusive innovations

This chapter reviews the possible contributions of inclusive innovation, i.e. innovations that support the welfare and entrepreneurship opportunities of lower-income and excluded groups. It describes how several trends, ranging from the widespread uptake of mobile telephony to growing business interest in inclusive innovations, have created more favourable conditions for inclusive innovation. It explores the obstacles and market failures facing inclusive innovations across four dimensions: 1) the types and costs of inclusive innovations; 2) information about consumer needs; 3) access to expertise, knowledge and finance; and 4) market access conditions. Based on this description, it provides an overview of factors that facilitate scaling up inclusive innovations.

"Inclusive innovation" projects are initiatives that serve the welfare of lower-income groups, including poor and excluded groups. While growth dynamics have lifted many people out of poverty, they have not eliminated poverty and exclusion, which continue to affect millions of people. Inclusive innovation has therefore become an imperative for countries' socio-economic development, especially in emerging and developing economies. In 2010, an estimated 4.3 billion people – 62% of the world's population – lived on less than USD 5 per day (World Bank, 2014a). Exclusion and relative poverty are also challenges for advanced economies, and obstacles to growth opportunities for all economies (OECD, 2015a).

Inclusive innovation will only be successful if it reaches a much larger segment of the poor and excluded population than it currently does. Many innovations remain small in scale and scope. Scaling up innovation requires initiatives that are built around: 1) financially sustainable business models; and/or 2) participation by lower-income and excluded groups, thereby supporting their integration in the formal economy. Meeting this objective, however, is challenging. To begin with, in many countries the income levels of a large segment of the population are low, hindering citizens from taking advantage of innovation and new technologies. Second, companies lack adequate knowledge on the needs of poor populations. Third, the infrastructure itself – e.g. roads and distribution channels – is inadequate, making it costly for companies to serve poor customers. Nevertheless, information and communication technologies (ICTs) have offered new opportunities for inclusive innovation. Mobile banking services – such as M-PESA, a mobile phone-based money transfer and microfinance service operating in Kenya and other countries – are examples of products reaching "scale".

What are the characteristics of inclusive innovations? What factors enable "scale"? This chapter aims to define inclusive innovations, as well as outline the challenges and opportunities in scaling innovations to meet the needs of lower-income and excluded groups.

The chapter is structured as follows: Section 1 describes inclusive innovation and the ways in which technology, business and policy trends support it. Section 2 focuses on the characteristics of inclusive innovation compared to innovation that does not specifically supply lower-income and excluded groups. Section 3 discusses factors that support scaling up inclusive innovations. Section 4 concludes.

1. The context of inclusive innovation

1.1. Definitions

Inclusive innovations improve the welfare of lower-income and, more broadly, excluded groups. Inclusive innovations have different dimensions, detailed below.

"Pro-inclusive innovations" often modify existing technologies, products or services to supply lower and middle-income groups. Among them, "frugal" innovations allow setting lower unit product prices by preserving only the most critical functionalities, while retaining core quality characteristics. The lower price allows lower-income groups to purchase those innovations.

Examples of pro-inclusive innovations include the Tata Nano (in the goods category), a low-cost, no-frills car produced in India, and Narayana Health, which provides lower-cost heart surgery thanks to standardised procedures allowing for extended use of unskilled labour for all tasks that do not require a doctor's intervention.

Many different actors, including micro, small and medium enterprises, large domestic corporations, multinational enterprises, state enterprises and not-for-profit corporations, have introduced pro-inclusive innovations. Business model innovations in particular are critical to inclusive innovations. Table 1.1 provides examples.

Table 1.1. **Examples of pro-inclusive and grassroots innovations**

	Nature of innovation		
	Service innovation		Product innovation
Pro-inclusive innovation	**Empresas Públicas de Medellín** A utility company providing energy and water services. Low-income users can use prepaid cards to pay for the service according to their cash flow. Households do not pay fixed installation costs. **Innovation:** Pay-per-use method. **Operator:** Public utility company. **Sector:** Energy and water. **Country:** Colombia. **Scale:** 43 000 low-income users have been connected since implementation in 2007.	**Narayana Health** One of India's largest healthcare services providers, Narayana Health offers low-cost cardiac surgeries and other healthcare services to the poor. It also caters to isolated communities via telemedicine. **Innovation:** Business process innovations aimed at decreasing surgery costs. Use of ICTs to establish healthcare centres in remote locations for poor rural communities. **Operator:** Private corporation. **Sector:** Healthcare. **Country:** India. **Scale:** 6 200 beds are spread across 23 hospitals in 14 cities (up from an initial 300 beds in 2001).	**MoneyMaker irrigation pump** Low-cost manpowered irrigation pumps. **Innovation:** No electricity or fuel is required for functioning and operating cost is lower. **Operator:** US-based NGO (KickStart). **Sector:** Agriculture. **Country:** Kenya, Mali, Tanzania. **Scale:** the pumps are distributed in local shops and sold to other NGOs for wider diffusion in the three countries.
Grassroots innovation	**Honey Bee Network** The Honey Bee Network links grassroots innovators from low-income groups. **Innovation:** the Network has developed an extensive database documenting innovations by the poorest, including in agricultural practices (e.g. natural pesticides), machinery and other sectors. The aim is to foster the diffusion of knowledge to a wider group of potential users. The Honey Bee Network also supports the protection of inventors' intellectual property and the commercialisation of marketable innovations by connecting informal innovators with formal institutions, including universities and public research institutions. **Sector:** All sectors relevant to low-income groups' livelihood. **Country:** India; similar networks in China and other countries. **Scale:** The Honey Bee Network led to the creation of India's National Innovation Foundation, an autonomous body aimed at providing institutional support to grassroots innovation. The Network's newsletter is printed in seven Indian languages. **Grassroots involvement:** The poor are the innovators and are recognised as such. They determine the conditions of use of their creation, as well as its eventual commercialisation and scale-up.		**Sanitary napkin-making machine** A low-cost sanitary napkin-making machine that produces affordable sanitary pads for very poor women. **Innovation:** improves women's health and provides them with economic activity. **Sector:** Health and manufacturing. **Country:** India. **Scale:** Present in 1 300 villages in 23 states across India and developing abroad. **Grassroots involvement:** the product was developed by an uneducated worker. India's National Innovation Foundation helped him apply for intellectual property rights and provided the means for the innovation to reach scale.

Source: www.safaricom.co.ke and The Economist (2012) for M-PESA; Suárez Franco, C.F. (2010) for Empresas Públicas de Medellín; Kothandaraman, P. and S. Mookerjee (2008) and www.narayanahealth.org for Narayana Health; OECD (2013) and www.kickstart.org for the MoneyMaker irrigation pump.

"Grassroots innovations" are inclusive innovations emphasising the empowerment of lower-income groups (Heeks et al., 2013).[1] While they are undertaken by the poor, they can be supported by other actors in the innovation system, including universities, non-governmental organisations (NGOs) and private firms. Poor populations can be involved through minor roles (e.g. as product distributors) or more extensive ones (e.g. as joint producers).[2] Grassroots innovation is also closely related to innovation in the informal economy. Examples of grassroots innovations include the well-known Honey Bee Network (Table 1.1 and Box 3.6) and the sanitary napkin-making machine.

Inclusive innovation often features additional characteristics. Professor Raghunath Anant Mashelkar, chairman of the National Innovation Foundation of India and president of the Global Research Alliance, defines it as "any innovation that leads to affordable access of quality goods and services creating livelihood opportunities for the excluded population, primarily at the base of the pyramid, and on a long-term sustainable basis with a significant outreach" (Mashelkar, 2013). This definition, paraphrased below, identifies five core characteristics:

- **Affordable access:** affordability depends on where individuals are positioned along the economic pyramid, the objective being to serve lower-income people through "extreme reduction" in production and distribution costs.
- **Sustainability:** affordable long-term access should rely on market mechanisms, without continued government support.
- **Quality goods and services and livelihood opportunities:** inclusive innovation is not about developing lower-quality products for those who cannot afford quality, but rather about providing better quality to improve their quality of life. This is strongly contingent on innovation, since providing high quality at a low price requires introducing new products, rather than adapting existing ones.
- **Access to the excluded population:** depending on specific national and social contexts, as well as the policy objectives, inclusive innovation should primarily benefit the poor, the disabled, migrants, women, the elderly, certain ethnic groups, etc.
- **Significant outreach:** true inclusion can only be realised if the benefits of inclusive innovation reach a large scale, i.e. a significant portion of the population stands to benefit from specific inclusive innovations.

Defining the target group of "inclusive" innovations depends on national policy contexts. It is even more complex from a global perspective encompassing developing, emerging and advanced economies, where the poorest have very different income levels. An innovation that is accessible to the poorest in advanced economies may only be accessible to the emerging middle classes – rather than the poor – in emerging and developing countries. Innovations such as the Tata Nano – known as the world's cheapest car – and Narayana Health's healthcare services (described in Table 1.1) fall into this category, yet are often cited as examples of inclusive innovations, for two reasons. *First*, these products are potentially relevant to serving the needs of the poorest in advanced countries. *Second* – similarly to inclusive innovations aimed at the poorest – their objective is to reach groups of people with lower incomes. Hence, it is relevant to include them in an analysis aiming to identify policy lessons on inclusive innovations.

This chapter will therefore focus on innovations that provide opportunities to the poor and lower-income and excluded groups in developing and emerging economies.[3] These include mobile phone services, fertilisers and other basic products supporting small-scale agriculture and supply services from which the poor are often excluded.

1.2. Country characteristics

The specific characteristics of poverty shape national priorities with regard to inclusive innovation:

- **Poverty's impact on rural populations:** more generally, poverty's geographic distribution determines certain needs (e.g. those of agricultural communities) and costs (e.g. those of transportation to remote markets). It also influences the number of different markets – often limited in size and with specific local demands, posing potential challenges for delivering certain types of inclusive innovations.

- **The population distribution across income groups:** where extreme poverty is widespread and markets are poorly developed, market-based inclusive innovations mechanisms face larger obstacles. The size of adjacent higher-income groups can help develop opportunities for cross-financing models, whereby the poorest pay a very low price, which is compensated by the higher price paid by the moderately poor of marginally higher income.

- **The overall national market size:** especially if accompanied by substantial economic growth, a relatively larger market can provide incentives for foreign multinational corporations in particular to supply it with innovations.

Box 1.1 describes poverty characteristics across five economies: China, Colombia, India, Indonesia and South Africa.

> ### Box 1.1. **Poverty in China, Colombia, India, Indonesia and South Africa**
>
> The **share of the population living in poverty varies substantially** among the five countries, although it is sensitive to the measure used. Based on a common threshold of constant 2005 USD 5 per day at purchasing power parity (PPP), 90% of Indonesia's population and 96% of India's population is poor, compared with 68% in China, 49% in Colombia and 62% in South Africa. Extreme poverty affects a large share of the population in each of the five countries and is particularly prevalent in India, Indonesia and South Africa.
>
> The **geography of poverty differs as well**. Poverty touches mostly rural populations in India (71%) and China (73%). In Indonesia, virtually half of the poor (52%) are urban dwellers; the other half live in rural areas. With the exception of Indonesia, population groups living in extreme poverty (less than USD 1.25 per day) are mostly rural.
>
> Finally, the **poor (i.e. those living on less than USD 5 per day) are not a homogenous group, and their distribution across the poverty scale** varies. In Colombia, more than half of the poor earn above USD 2.50 per day. In India, on the contrary, the majority (84%) of the poor live on less than USD 2.50 per day: thus, they are not only more numerous, but much poorer than their Colombian counterparts, which means that the pricing strategies of similar inclusive innovations will need to be adapted. In Indonesia and South Africa, the distribution of poverty is also weighted towards extreme poverty, albeit to a lesser extent: two-thirds of the poor live on less than USD 2.50 per day. In China, 53% of the poor live on less than USD 2.50 per day.
>
> *Note:* Income segments are expressed in 2005 PPP. For India and Indonesia, national distribution is based on an aggregated Lorenz curve from original rural and urban distribution. Information is for 2010 for Colombia and Indonesia, 2009 for China and India and 2008 for South Africa.
> *Source:* PovcalNet, Development Research Group, World Bank, http://iresearch.worldbank.org/PovcalNet/index.htm?0 (accessed on 30 May 2014). Data are based on primary household survey data obtained from government statistical agencies and World Bank country departments.

1.3. Opportunities for inclusive innovation

Several ongoing trends in technology, business, policy and macroeconomics create wider opportunities for successful inclusive innovation models compared to the past.

ICTs and other technologies

ICTs in general – and mobile phones in particular – have provided an opportunity for leapfrogging critical infrastructural shortcomings. By successfully connecting a much larger number of the poor to the mobile phone network, they have served as a platform for several "inclusive innovations" in the areas of health and education (Box 1.2), as well as a platform for activities involving the poor in agriculture and fishing. ICTs also have the potential to further improve opportunities for mobile banking (OECD, 2013): as the cost of providing mobile services only involves developing the applications, the service itself can be distributed for free on a wide scale.

Box 1.2. Examples of mobile health and education applications

Child Count+, Kenya: this application registers pregnant women and children under five and collects basic information on their health to organise visits by health workers.

Tamil Nadu Health Watch, India: this disease surveillance system, introduced after the tsunami in 2004, provides instant links between primary health centres in four districts to enable health experts and programme managers to co-ordinate activities more effectively and allocate resources more efficiently. Use of mobile phones allows health workers, even in remote areas, to report disease incidence data immediately to health officials, speeding up their ability to respond.

Project Masiluleke, South Africa: the project increases the volume of patients who are screened for HIV/AIDS and receive information on prevention and treatment. It sends out about 1 million messages per day and covers nearly all country mobile phone users in a year. The project is supported by the Praekelt Foundation, the PopTech innovation network, LifeLine Southern Africa (the government-backed provider of the helpline), iTEACH, Frog Design and MTN.

Text to Change, South Africa: this application uses mobile phone technology, specifically interactive and incentive-based SMS messaging, to send and receive information to educate, engage and empower people on issues related to well-being, e.g. health care, education and economic development. Text to Change also has campaigns in South America.

Virtual University of Pakistan (VUP): this ICT-based university currently offering 17 degree programmes uses the national telecommunications infrastructure and delivers lectures asynchronously through satellite broadcast TV channels, with interaction provided over the Internet.

Source: OECD (2013), based on Melhem and Tandon (2009) and www.sehatfirst.com for Sehat First; Adler and Uppal (2008) for Tamil Nadu Health Watch; Zhenwei Qiang et al. (2012) for Project Masiluleke; CHAI/HP, Zhenwei Qiang et al. (2012) for WelTel, Child Count+; CII (2011) for ReMeDi; Zhenwei Qiang et al. (2011) for ProjectMind and text2teach; Baggaley and Belawati (2010) for the VUP.

However, it should be noted that "virtual" services will not be a bridge in all cases – the delivery of physical goods requires a physical infrastructure. Moreover, the benefits around mobile markets have come from competition including lower prices for people to first get telephones and service. The more governments encourage competition the more services will evolve from second-generation (2G) to fourth-generation wireless telephone technology with all the associated benefits of inexpensive smartphones and the services they enable including for lower-income and excluded groups.

The growing number of new ICT-based business approaches provides novel opportunities for inclusive innovation. A recent innovation in financing microcredit is online microlending, where individual investors provide loan capital via the Internet. One example is Kiva.org, a not-for-profit organisation operating an online platform where individuals can lend money (from USD 25) to entrepreneurs of their choice in developing countries. The platform provides "profiles" of applicants' projects, which have been screened by Kiva's partners, international microfinance institutions (MFIs) and social businesses. Kiva has disbursed more than 678 000 loans since its inception in 2005, with an average loan size of USD 415 (Kiva, 2014).

Other frontier technologies can also support inclusive innovations, including the Foldscope (Box 1.3) and the use of solar power to provide more poor people with access to electricity.

> **Box 1.3. The Foldscope: A pro-inclusive innovation for inclusive science**
>
> The Foldscope is a folded-paper microscope offering 2 000 times magnification. While its power and quality equate those of desktop microscopes worth thousands of dollars, it can be manufactured for under USD 0.50 using three-dimensional (3D) printing. The microscope is made of cheap and abundant material (paper) and requires minimal assembly skills, keeping production costs low. Designed by Professor Manu Prakash of Stanford University, the Foldscope is being tested in India and Uganda as a diagnostic tool for malaria and other acute bacterial diseases. The Foldscope was designed as a platform technology: it aims to bring science to the masses and is adapted to different local contexts and uses. To this end, it is resilient and portable and does not require any power source. To achieve the Foldscope's objectives, the creators are giving away 10 000 microscopes to researchers and citizens around the world to test on potential applications. As of April 2014, they had received over 10 000 applications, including from a Mongolian farmer wishing to use the Foldscope to monitor milk quality and from the Canadian Space agency to use as a miniaturised microscope to send micro-organisms into space.
>
> Source: Markoff (2014); Dobrovolny (2014); Foldscope.com (2014).

Data-driven innovation

Increasingly, large volumes of (digital) data, known as "big data", are available to governments, businesses, researchers and citizens groups. Data sources include, but are not limited to, mobile phones, social media and administrative records. Data and analytics are enabling new insights and the significant improvement or development of new products, processes, organisational methods and markets (i.e. "data-driven innovation") (see OECD, forthcoming).

Such data-driven innovation has the potential to help address the urging needs of developing and emerging economies and can give countries the capacity to "leap-frog" in critical development areas such as agriculture, finance and transports (see Gerdon and Reimsbach-Kounatze, forthcoming). In the field of agriculture, data analytics can improve the work of farmers through information, forecasting and evaluation in particular on the local level. The International Center for Tropical Agriculture (CIAT), for instance, developed a climate-smart, site-specific recommendation engine for Colombian rice farmers, which is based on meteorological data and seasonal forecasts.

Microfinance and policy

Substantial experimentation and favourable experiences with microfinance provide opportunities for stabilising poor people's revenue streams (McIntosh, 2011). Microfinance can also support investments and risk management by grassroots entrepreneurs, and has been found to positively affect business size (Angelucci et al., 2014). However, traditional microfinance models need adapting to suit the needs of grassroots entrepreneurs. For instance, rigid and/or short-term repayment schedules are ill-suited to farmers, since agricultural production cycles are commonly longer than in other industries (Dalla Pellegrina, 2011). Introducing a more flexible repayment schedule – which also offers a longer return on investment – can have positive impacts on business investment and creation (Field et al., 2013).

Successful pro-poor policy initiatives in the form of cash transfer programmes and extensive experience with public-private partnerships can also provide novel policy models supporting inclusive innovation. Based on such experience, pioneer innovators can develop hybrid models that make the involvement of the private sector in public activities much more viable by offering business opportunities.

Business and macroeconomics

The growing importance of emerging markets, including China, India and Indonesia, also contributes substantially to orienting business interests towards innovations serving lower-income markets. Prahalad and Hart (2002) have popularised the business case for social-value creation. They introduced the concept of the "bottom of the pyramid" (BoP), further developed in Prahalad (2005). The International Finance Corporation (IFC) and the World Resources Institute (Hammond et al., 2007) provide a systematic analysis of the BoP across different countries and sectors. They estimated that in 2002, the 4 billion people living in poverty constituted a USD 5 trillion global consumer market, of which the 5 economies of China, Colombia, India, Indonesia and South Africa represented USD 3.2 trillion. Another reason why large multinationals devote more attention to these markets is to build brand loyalties among the poor, as these consumers will likely belong to higher-income consumer groups in the future. Yet another factor facilitating the development of inclusive innovation initiatives is their greater emphasis on corporate social responsibility. The success of fair trade products, for example, reveals a willingness on the part of consumers in developed economies to support poverty alleviation efforts.[4]

2. In what ways are inclusive innovations different?

Inclusive innovations are not characterised by their incremental or radical nature – or whether they are new to the firm, the market or the world – but rather by their consumers and producers, that are different from other innovations. Inclusive – i.e. pro-inclusive and grassroots – innovations can be compared to standard innovations designed by entrepreneurs for higher-income markets.[5] Inclusive innovations differ from standard innovations aimed at middle or higher-income markets according to the following criteria: 1) type and costs of innovation; 2) information about consumer needs; 3) access to expertise, knowledge and financing; and 4) market conditions for innovators. These criteria point to the different challenges facing inclusive innovations.

2.1. Type and costs of inclusive innovations

The types and impacts of inclusive innovations differ from those of stylised innovations, as show in Table 1.2 (Column 1). This applies to both pro-inclusive innovations (innovations produced by companies, NGOs, and so on, for the poor) and grassroots innovations (innovation for the poor by the poor). Demand for pro-inclusive and grassroots innovations is more sensitive to price, and often more volatile. Lower education levels among the poor can also reduce uptake. In Colombia, for instance, the gap in the number of years of schooling between the first and fifth income quintile in 2011 was about 6.3 years (Center for Distributive, Labor and Social Studies [CEDLAS] and the World Bank, 2014).

Where the types of innovations are concerned, certain products are relatively more important for lower-income groups than others and their development should be a priority if the objective is to serve those groups. These include not only food (as suggested by the Engel curve, which shows that poorer households devote a larger share of their income to basic needs), but also public services such as health, transport and infrastructure, to which the poor often do not have access. Again in Colombia, 18% of the lowest-income population did not have access to water and 53% lacked access to sewage in 2012 (CEDLAS and the World Bank, 2014). By contrast, innovative products in domains that are less critical will be more difficult to finance via co-financing by the poor.

Unlike formal research and development processes, the grassroots innovation approach relies on needs-based user experimentation. It often leads to incremental innovations – some of which are adaptations of existing innovations. Grassroots innovations, however, are not necessarily non-technological and can often benefit from technology: one of the critical roles of the Honey Bee Network is to connect grassroots innovators with scientists and engineers to help develop their innovations.

Pro-inclusive innovations can also be highly technological, as illustrated by Protoprint, a pro-inclusive innovation bridging the gap between "high-level" innovation and inclusive innovation (Box 1.4).

Box 1.4. Linking high-level innovation with pro-inclusive innovation: Protoprint

In India, garbage collection is done at the dumpsite and garbage pickers sell raw plastic to intermediaries, often receiving less than USD 1 per day. Protoprint, an Indian company created by 2 MIT D-Lab students, developed a low-cost technology enabling garbage pickers to transform reclaimed plastic into 3D printing filament, increasing their income 15 times for a given amount of plastic collected. Protoprint has created two low-cost, easy-to-use machines that will eventually allow producing the printing filament: the Flakerbot, which shreds high density polyethylene plastic, and the RefilBot, which cooks the plastic flakes and extrudes a 3D printing filament. Protoprint currently has a pilot "filament lab" in Pune and partners with SWaCH (Solid Waste Collection and Handling), a co-operative of self-employed waste pickers. Product development is still ongoing and filaments are being tested on a variety of printers. Wider diffusion of the product is slated for early 2015.

Source: www.protoprint.in (accessed on 6 November 2014); Mashelkar (2014).

When it comes to inclusive innovation, substantial costs linked to providing products to the poor can arise. The lack of access to electricity constrains the types of products available to them and requires innovative approaches to adapting products. Shortcomings in infrastructure further add to the costs of delivery in remote areas. For example, while 79% of roads were paved in OECD countries in 2011, only 53% were paved in middle-income economies and 21% in low-income economies (World Bank Development Indicators, 2014). These shortcomings in infrastructure quality compared with OECD countries affect poor and rural populations in particular. Table 1.2 describes in more detail the costs of providing innovations and provides examples.

2.2. Consumer needs

Obtaining information about consumer needs is particularly challenging for most pro-inclusive innovators. First, there is a larger gap between producers and consumers, who are often located in remote areas or urban slums. Second, informal and limited records of consumption patterns (which are also affected by volatile incomes) require specific approaches to information gathering. The example of the Tata Nano illustrates that understanding consumers' needs does not simply relate to price. The product was less successful than expected not only because of the price increase,[6] but also because of safety shortcomings and – more importantly – the fact that it was marketed as a "cheap" car, which did not appeal to lower-income consumers in search of good-quality products.

"Standard" innovators have easier access to consumer information because 1) the distance between users and producers is shorter than it is for pro-inclusive innovators; and 2) producers have access to more information on consumers drawn from consumption preferences (e.g. through phone surveys, analysis of online consumption behaviour or registered purchasing behaviour).

Grassroots innovators are often direct users of their innovations, and hence have better knowledge about their needs than outsiders. They may, however, lack knowledge about needs elsewhere, thus missing opportunities to diffuse their invention more widely. The Honey Bee Network in India supports many grassroots innovations (e.g. a time-saving pedal-powered washing machine that requires no electricity) answering specific local requirements.

Partnerships between small/grassroots entrepreneurs and large companies (which have the advantage of scale, but lack insight into poor consumers' needs) can be relevant to developing tailored products both at the local and larger scale. Governments can play a role in fostering such partnerships (Prabhu, 2014). Constructing platforms for collecting examples of successful developments of inclusive innovation projects, as well as devising innovative ways of involving the poor in the product development process (as with some types of grassroots innovations), can be helpful. The Massachusetts Institute of Technology's D-Lab (MIT D-Lab) in the United States channels researchers' creativity towards pro-inclusive innovation and collaborates closely with low-income groups in developing countries to adapt innovations to local needs.

2.3. Access to expertise, knowledge and finance

The conditions for accessing expertise and knowledge differ across standard, pro-inclusive and grassroots innovators (whose generally better knowledge of user needs compared to pro-inclusive innovators gives them a critical advantage). However, grassroots

Table 1.2. **Characteristics and examples of inclusive innovations compared with standard innovations**

	Types of innovation and their impact	Cost of providing innovations
Stylised "standard" innovations	• Opportunities provided for radical and incremental types of innovation and the full range of product, process, marketing and organisational innovations. Demand and supply conditions allow exploring a variety of demands. • Demand for individual firm characterised by volatility depending on income trends, competition and consumer uptake – but often less dependent on overall market size for a given innovation and less prone to exogenous shocks. This is due to a) larger market size, with individual demand less of an overall driver; and b) consumers commonly having higher incomes. • Higher incomes provide opportunities for consumption of products with longer-term benefits and corresponding investments. • Consumers are often better informed about product benefits and uses, allowing for more informed consumption (e.g. of health-related services).	• Larger opportunities for innovation development compared to inclusive innovators, as public goods – infrastructure, electricity, security and transport services – provide adequate market infrastructure.

Inclusive innovations	• Demand requires innovations that substitute for absent public services (e.g. in health, education, infrastructure/ transport and communication services).
	   ❖ **Amanz Abantu** (South Africa) is a company specialising in providing water to undersupplied low-income communities by installing pay-per-use pumps in accessible locations.
	• Demand for innovations is characterised by uncertainty: new products often create new markets, whose prospects are hard to evaluate, and consumers rely on cash flows, which are subject to shocks (e.g. due to lack of work, illness and lack of insurance), for consumption.[1]
	   ❖ **The Aishwarya solar lantern** (India) failed because its pricing scheme (high upfront lump-sum payment) was not compatible with the demand characteristics (volatile income). On the contrary, pay-per-use strategies are more adapted to the poor: **the EPM energy company** (Colombia) increased its outreach to the lowest-income groups by introducing a prepaid card system.
	• Grassroots innovations need to emphasise economic activities relevant to the poor, such as agriculture, waste collection and handicrafts.
	   ❖ **Tedcor** (South Africa) trains entrepreneurs from disadvantaged backgrounds to provide effective waste management. Tedcor obtains waste treatment contracts with municipalities and subcontracts tasks to these small businesses. The company thus ensures regular demand for the entrepreneurs' services, also extending waste collection services to previously underserved areas – made possible by a lower overall cost of the waste management services.
	   ❖ **The Honey Bee Network database** (India) records agricultural innovations, such as techniques to improve productivity and natural pest control.
	• Inclusive innovation provides returns to consumers; for grassroots innovations, additional contributions stem from integrating the poor into economic activities.
	   ❖ **The Jayaashree Industries sanitary napkin-making machine** (India) creates economic activity and income for women; it improves their health and the welfare of their families.
	• The constrained budgets of the poor entail a low willingness and ability to pay for products and services without immediate tangible benefits. Additionally, they have less awareness about products' benefits and uses than higher-income groups, leading to low uptake. Education efforts and alternative financing schemes are required in these cases.
	   ❖ In the case of the **Jayaashree Industries sanitary napkin-making machine** (India), ignorance and taboo were barriers to uptake of the sanitary products. Relying on word-of-mouth and women's self-help groups to spread information on the products' health benefits solved this issue.
		• Lack of baseline conditions – e.g. limited access to electricity – limit access to possible technologies for the poor (resulting in lower range of viable products compared to standard innovations) or make development costlier, thereby reducing uptake by imposing the need to invent around a challenge.
		• Lack of infrastructure raises costs ("poverty premium") of supplying the lowest-income market with products (compared to other markets of standard innovations); often "difficult-to-reach" markets (notably slums and remote rural areas) increase prices charged for products.
		   ❖ **The MFI Fincomun (Mexico) partnered with Bimbo, a producer of bakery goods** with a large distribution network, so that the microfinance agents could take advantage of Bimbo supply trucks to reach potential clients (small low-income shop owners) that would be costly to reach otherwise.
		   ❖ Grassroots innovator **Jayaashree Industries** (India) sells the sanitary napkin-making machines to local self-help groups across India instead of producing them centrally, thereby avoiding large transportation costs.

Table 1.2. **Characteristics and examples of inclusive innovations compared with standard innovations** (cont.)

	Types of innovation and their impact	Cost of providing innovations

Differential policy approaches for inclusive innovation	• Ensure regulatory impediments do not prohibit or constrain innovations serving the poor (particularly with regard to public services).
	  ❖ **Amanz Abantu** (South Africa): one of the main challenges facing the private water company was regulatory barriers, i.e. considerable red-tape for tendering to government projects and controversy on the private provision of water.
	  ❖ **M-PESA**, a mobile payment company that became virtually ubiquitous in Kenya, could not develop successfully in South Africa due to regulatory impediments (stricter regulation to prevent money laundering).
	• Facilitate access to training and capital to improve contributions.
	  ❖ **The National Innovation Foundation** (India) offers technical and financial support for developing grassroots innovations.
	• Developing credit options to smooth consumption patterns will also support catering to this market by providing firms with more stable income through predictable demand.
	  ❖ **Microsaving and microcredit** opportunities render the very poor less vulnerable to income shocks.
	• Options for cross-subsidising consumption and other ways of lowering costs will be inevitable for some types of consumption (particularly for lowest-income groups).
	  ❖ **Ziqitza Ambulances** (India) charge patients based on their income. Cross-subsidisation allows them to extend services to the poorest.
	• Training/providing consumer information (e.g. through information campaigns and group training to share information with others) is critical to the uptake of relevant products.
		• Product provision should be devised in a way that either does not require basic infrastructure (making mobile phone-based services particularly attractive) or simultaneously supplies infrastructure (e.g. by developing joint delivery processes).
		  ❖ **ReMeDi – remote medical diagnostics** (India) uses existing Internet kiosks to set up remote consultation with doctors for low-income patients in isolated areas.
		• Continued efforts to provide basic infrastructure can raise opportunities for inclusive innovations, as will efforts – possibly based on alternative approaches (e.g. solar power) – to provide access to electricity.
		  ❖ **Terrasys Energy** (Indonesia) provides electricity to hard-to-reach communities using run-of the river hydropower stations.

Note: Further information on specific examples is provided in Appendix 1 of Paunov and Lavison (2014) or in a corresponding box, if indicated.

1. The poor have many other necessities to satisfy in the short run (Banerjee and Duflo, 2010). The result is that poor individuals' consumption and investment decisions tend to be persistently inefficient. Other papers that treat this problem include Banerjee and Mullainathan (2010); Banerjee et al. (2010); Tarozzi et al. (2011); Duflo, Kremer and Robinson (2010); and Ashraf, Karlan and Yin (2006).

innovators often face greater difficulty in finding the technical expertise they lack in-house and have more limited access to external knowledge sources. It is worth noting the parallels with open-innovation initiatives: Von Hippel (2005) emphasises that lead users with expertise are critical of open innovation. The stereotypical users are leading experts in their fields, e.g. skilled computer programmers (for the much-cited example of the open-source innovator community), but also extreme sports fanatics whose intimate knowledge of specific problems gives them higher capacities than the sports companies to design customised products. Grassroots innovators also have deep knowledge of the challenges they face, but lack the expertise. The first column of Table 1.3 shows the major differences among the different kinds of innovators, illustrated by policy examples.

Inclusive innovators have access to different financing conditions than grassroots innovators (Table 1.3, Column 2). These challenges compound the already restricted financing opportunities available to them in developing and emerging economies. As Figure 1.1 shows, the share of the poor holding an account in a financial institution is much lower than among higher-income groups. The size of the gap varies across countries: in Colombia, individuals with an income in the top 60% were almost 3 times more likely to hold an account at a financial institution than the remaining 40%. In South Africa, the gap is less important: borrowing rates tend to be modest, incomes are generally low and

Table 1.3. **Particularities of grassroots innovations compared with standard and pro-inclusive innovations**

	Access to expertise and knowledge	Access to financing	Market conditions
Stylised standard and pro-inclusive innovators	• Possess greater expertise (absorptive capacity) on the technologies available "in-house". ❖ **Terrasys Energy** (Indonesia) uses state-of-the-art hydroelectricity production techniques to produce electricity locally in remote areas. • Have wider opportunities to connect to expertise at other firms, universities and public research institutions. • Pro-inclusive innovators may face a greater challenge in tapping into user expertise, given the larger distance between users and developers. ❖ The household appliance company **Haier** (China) developed a network of franchises in rural areas and tapped into franchisees' knowledge to adapt its products to end users.	• Financial resources for innovation are determined by market trends, i.e. economic trends, consumer uptake, and competitors. While some volatility exists regarding investments, it is lower than for grassroots innovators, since risks are generally not "personal". • Standard innovators have greater opportunities for receiving loans from formal financial institutions than pro-inclusive innovators due to the following: ❖ There are fewer delays/risk regarding product uptake; the larger scale of future production allows greater opportunities for larger loans or investments (particularly where innovations target specific small markets). ❖ Some opportunities exist for risk financing, including venture capital and other types of innovation financing. • Further differences for pro-inclusive innovators arise because of the following: ❖ Product uptake is longer/riskier, since these innovations often create new markets with larger information asymmetries (compared to standard innovators). ❖ The potentially low scale of the future market and uptake limits the potential for standard loans. ❖ Opportunities for non-standard financing include impact investment (financial resources for inclusive innovation), but future opportunities should be explored.	• Firms' formal status: ❖ Facilitates access to public services – including public support policies – required for operations and innovation activities. ❖ Provides wider opportunities for contracting with suppliers and consumers. ❖ Offers opportunities for protecting the innovations created, particularly by securing intellectual property (IP), which in turn can facilitate expanding activities and up-scaling (e.g. patents can facilitate access to finance by signalling the value of a company's invention). ❖ Lowers exposure to various infrastructural constraints (access to finance, costs of providing innovation or connection to knowledge networks). ❖ The pro-inclusive innovator **Moladi** (South **Africa**) patented its re-usable plastic moulds that allow building fast and durable housing for and by low-income people.

Table 1.3. **Particularities of grassroots innovations compared with standard and pro-inclusive innovations** (cont.)

	Access to expertise and knowledge	Access to financing	Market conditions

Grassroots innovators	• Users are by definition involved in the innovation process (to different degrees, however; see Table 1.1).
	• Expertise is largely related to experience/knowledge of problems and specific circumstances.
	• The informal nature of business entails limited knowledge of technologies and absorptive capacities, and fewer opportunities for tapping into "knowledge networks".
	  ❖ The inventor of **the Jayaashree Industries** sanitary napkin-making machine (India) experienced difficulties in obtaining information from firms in the formal sector, delaying the development of his product.
		• Their financial resources are determined partly by market trends, but also by investment opportunities dependent on "personal" conditions.
		• Volatility can be substantial and investments are needed to improve personal living conditions. As a result, subsistence-driven activities may reduce willingness to experiment and take risks.
		• The lending conditions are challenging because:
		  ❖ Informality makes contract enforcement difficult, and thus reduces credit opportunities.
		  ❖ Product uptake is longer/riskier, since these innovations often create new markets.
		  ❖ The potentially low scale of many future markets, combined with the correspondingly low loan requirements and opportunities, limits the potential for standard loans.
		  ❖ Opportunities for non-standard financing include impact investment (financial resources for inclusive innovation), but future opportunities should be explored.
			• Firms/innovators' informal status:
			  ❖ Makes accessing public services more difficult.
			  ❖ Reduces contracting to informal settings, raising costs and leading to potentially less optimal agreements.
			  ❖ Provides limited opportunities for protecting inventions, exposing innovators to a greater risk of theft and desire to keep inventions secret, thereby reducing opportunities for scale; possible side-selling can also lower uptake (if lower-quality alternatives are provided).
			  ❖ Entails higher exposure to infrastructural constraints, increasing supply costs.
			• For the poorest groups, time available for engaging in activities might be reduced (e.g. if basic livelihood requires seeking drinking water, ensuring basic food supplies), limited opportunities for engaging in other economic activities.

Differential policy approaches for inclusive innovation	• Support intermediary institutions and other means of knowledge exchange to provide technical expertise to grassroots innovators and information on the needs of the poor to pro-inclusive innovators.
	  ❖ The **China Innovation Network**, established in collaboration with the Honey Bee Network and the Tianjin University of Finance and Economics, aims to support grassroots innovations.
	• Stimulate/support research institutions that foster inclusive innovation.
	  ❖ The **MIT D-Lab** supports inclusive innovation from development to commercialisation by supplying technical expertise (e.g. the Creative Capacity Building programme for pro-inclusive entrepreneurs and open-source technologies for grassroots entrepreneurs).
	  ❖ The **Techpedia project of the Honey Bee Network** (India) promotes links between technology students and innovators in the informal sector.
	• Train the poor to build absorptive capacities.
		• Identify opportunities for small-scale activities, avoiding volatility and moral hazard; this points to a close connection with microfinance models.
		  ❖ The MFI **Swayam Krishi Sangam (SKS)** (India) partnered with Nokia and Bharti Airtel (services provider) to provide mobile phones, jointly with a microloan to pay for them in areas with no mobile phone penetration.
		• Explore novel social financing models for inclusive innovation that ensure efficient financial operations.
		• Major risk of uptake, combined with information challenges and the costs of supplying markets, requires support and funding beyond the initial product development stages (traditionally seen as the most critical phase).
		  ❖ The **India Inclusive Innovation Fund** pledged to spend 50% of its first investment on SMEs.
			• Investigate policy approaches relative to the informal sector aiming to better integrate informal activities by enhancing access to services, exploring opportunities for IP and addressing infrastructural constraints.
			  ❖ The **Oro Verde** co-operative (Colombia) supports traditional gold and platinum miners and helps them reach international markets at premium prices thanks to their ecological practices. Oro Verde uses IP to protect and promote its brand specificity.

Note: Further information on specific examples is provided in Appendix 1 of Paunov and Lavison (2014) or in a corresponding box, if indicated.

Figure 1.1. **Financial inclusion of the population (2011) (% age 15+)**

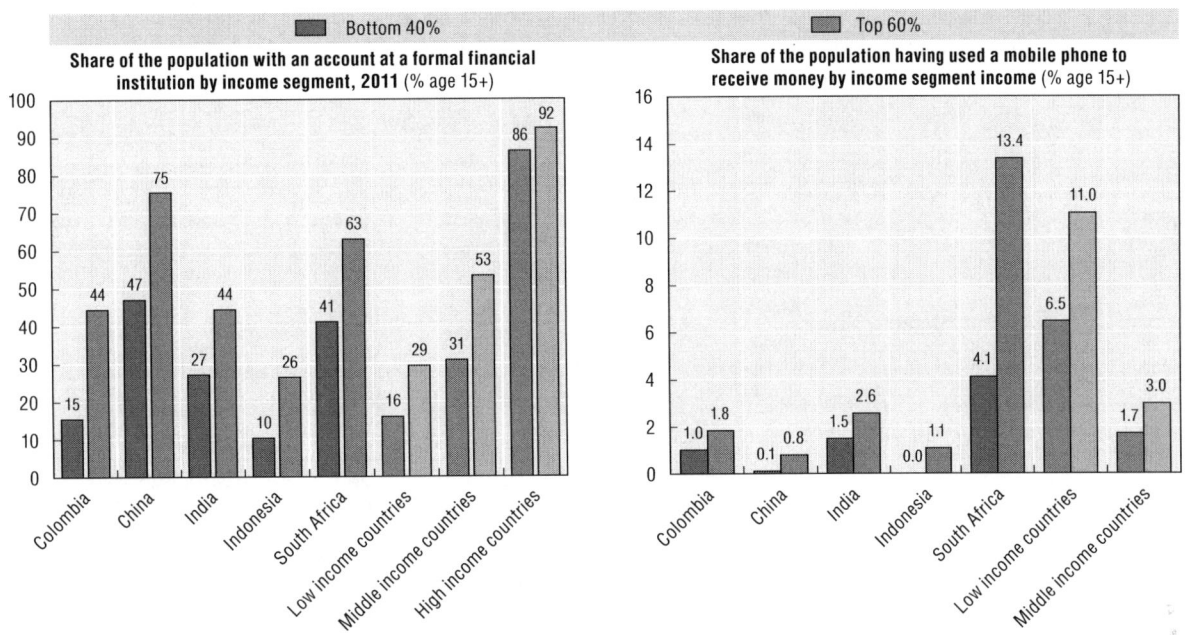

Note: "An account at a formal financial institution" includes all accounts (owned singly or with another person) held at a bank, credit union, another financial institution (e.g. co-operative or MFI), or the post office (if applicable); this category includes respondents who reported owning a debit card. The sample for India excludes the north-eastern states and remote islands, which combined represent around 10% of the total adult population. Unless otherwise noted, data for Indonesia include Timor-Leste through 1999. Low-income economies are those in which 2010 gross national income (GNI) per capita was USD 1 005 or less. Middle-income economies are those in which 2010 GNI per capita ranged between USD 1 006 and USD 12 275. High-income economies are those in which 2010 GNI per capita was USD 12 276 or more.
Source: Global Financial Inclusion (Global Findex) Database (World Bank, 2011), based on Demirgüç-Kunt and Klapper (2012).

volatile, and savings are limited. As a result, the lack of access to banking services is a major obstacle both to grassroots innovators and consumers. As a general rule, novel financial tools (e.g. mobile banking) are still only rarely used (Figure 1.1), with some exceptions: in Kenya, only 19% of the poorest 40% of the population had an account in a financial institution, but 53% used a mobile phone to receive money and 43% to send money (World Bank Global Financial Inclusion Database).

2.4. Market conditions for firms

As Table 1.3 (Column 3) shows, grassroots innovators face different market conditions than traditional and pro-inclusive innovators. Grassroots innovators often operate as informal businesses. Given their importance within national economies, however, policy makers would do well to foster innovation in their local context: in 2007, the informal economy amounted to 14.3% of gross domestic product (GDP) in China, 45.1% of GDP in Colombia, 25.6% in India, 20.9% in Indonesia and 31.7% in South Africa (Schneider et al., 2010). The informal sector employs 84% of the non-agricultural workforce in India, 60% in Colombia, 33% in South Africa (International Labour Organization [ILO], 2011) and 68% in Indonesia (OECD, 2015a). Most informal enterprises are small, with fewer than nine employees (IFC, 2013a). Companies in the informal sector face substantial obstacles, both financial – e.g. gaining access to external resources (IFC, 2013b) – and infrastructural – e.g. access to electricity. Nevertheless, the significant uptake of mobile phones (59% over 2006-11) among informal enterprises has a positive correlation with their sales (Paunov and Rollo, 2014).

The differential characteristics discussed above mean that the market for inclusive innovations is particularly difficult to enter. Innovators face larger uncertainty and information asymmetries, as well as larger sunk costs (since markets are often created from scratch and require infrastructure/ecosystem development to become profitable), all of which result in missed markets. Moreover, among the relatively large pool of potentially successful inclusive innovations that have been developed, few have managed to reach a large enough scale to make a sizeable impact.

3. What is the impact of inclusive innovations?

3.1. Scaling up

An innovation's scale depends on market segmentation or consumer location. Localisation can be critical (e.g. for agricultural activities) not only to improve local production techniques, but also to adapt them to specific rural contexts. Given their potential consumers' income and numbers, standard innovators may have better opportunities than inclusive innovators to attain production scale and product standardisation (since agriculture plays a lesser role and local specificities have less impact on products not typically required by the poor). Inclusive innovators, on the other hand, may face cost-based challenges, which ICT-based services (among others) can help address. This is because economies of scale for expanding ICT-based services are often very low.

In the absence of representative statistics, the evidence to date suggests that few cases have reached scale. Kubzansky, Cooper and Barbari (2011) surveyed 439 inclusive businesses and found that only 37% were commercially viable and had the potential to achieve scale. Only 13% were operating at scale, with operating volatile margins between 10% and 15%. Similarly, a detailed assessment of mobile healthcare applications shows substantial differences in scale (Figure 1.2). These numbers, however, do not necessarily point to higher failure rates for inclusive innovations, as standard innovators also show a substantial failure rate.

The type of innovation is very much a factor when it comes to scaling up. Reaching maximum scale depends strongly on demand – which will be quite low for localised products, but may involve millions of customers for broader-based services, e.g. mobile banking. Furthermore, product-level scaling is not an absolute necessity: the very process of designing local innovations to serve local needs may support an inherently small-scale market, while also contributing to poverty alleviation. One solution can consist in creating networks to explore opportunities to enhance uptake of localised solutions through customisation. In India, the Honey Bee Network helped license the Groundnut Digger – a groundnut-sorting machine developed by a farmer – to an entrepreneur for the purpose of cleaning beaches. Such networks are particularly relevant to the discussion of policy options supporting inclusive innovation (Chapter 3), as national-level support for small-scale projects is difficult to obtain, while policy support for reaching scale can be substantial.

As is the case for standard innovations, developing sustainability can vary across the various development stages, with greater risks at the early stages of the innovation process. M-PESA is an example of an initially not-for-profit inclusive innovation that reached commercial viability, as well as soft funding and government support, after several years of trial and error (Foster and Heeks, 2013). Drawing conclusions on the share of inclusive innovations that have successfully scaled up is arduous, since the main analysis to date is based on case studies. However, the fact that only a few of the cases (see Section 4.2.),

Figure 1.2. **Scale of mobile health applications in Haiti, India and Kenya, 2010 (number of unique users or transactions)**

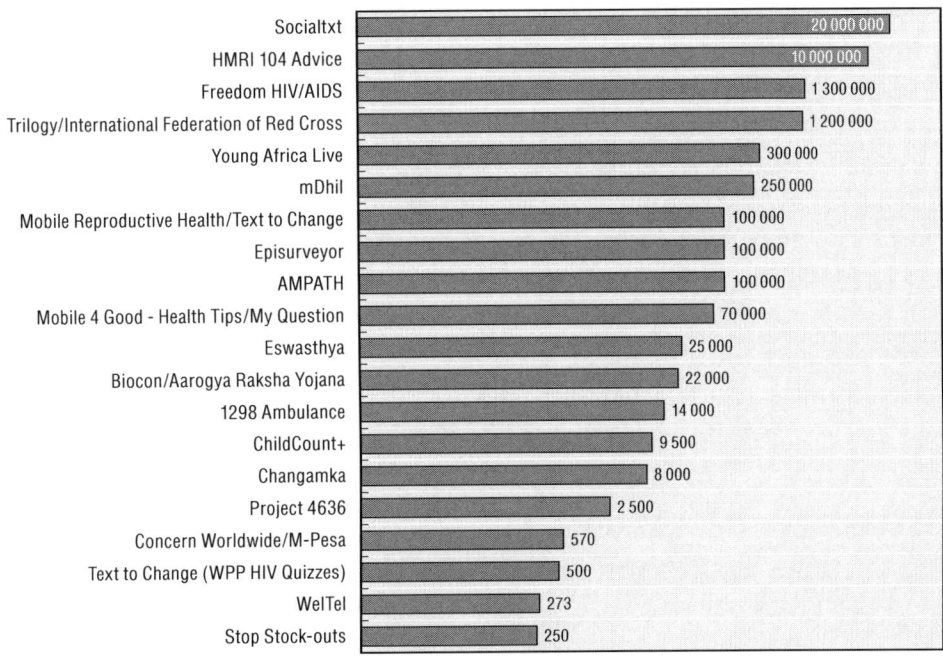

Source: Dahlberg research and analysis, quoted in Zhenwei Qiang et al. (2012).

even among the frequently quoted examples, have reached scale suggests it is a persistent challenge – a conclusion also reached at the OECD Symposium on Innovation for Inclusive Growth (OECD, 2014).

3.2. Success factors for scaling

Inclusive innovations that have scaled up successfully include mobile phones and some mobile services (such as M-PESA), several microfinance initiatives (discussed in Section 1.3), as well as Jaipur Foot, Fuel from the Fields and Narayana Health. This success has occurred for several reasons.

- The product responded to **strong demand**, as demonstrated by the poor's willingness to pay for such services. Mobile phones, for instance, were taken up even where electricity supply was a challenge, because communication needs were substantial. In 2013, mobile phone subscriptions per 100 inhabitants amounted to 89.4% in developing countries (International Telecommunication Union [ITU], 2014). Uptake among firms, including informal enterprises, was considerable (Paunov and Rollo, 2014). The mobile banking service M-PESA is another widely adopted product that answered strong demand.

- Successful innovators **invested in gaining a deep understanding of the requirements of the poor**, which can be achieved by involving them directly in innovation processes. Starting from the demand side (i.e. by observing consumer habits and stated needs) to design a product is an advanced way to include end users, which has driven the success of MFI initiatives and identified opportunities to include end users.

- **Developing profitable business models** was a priority. This process often involves multiple iterations, aimed at identifying opportunities for success, which might be described as "**thinking out of the box**". MFIs are a good example of how evaluating and experimenting with different models has helped build success. Innovative **pricing and financing strategies**, as well as modified business processes, have also proved critical. Tables 1.4 and 1.5 illustrate these issues. They show that while cost reduction was generally the main criterion, other factors (including ensuring product quality and the application's usefulness) were critical too. Cost effectiveness and profit-driven objectives have often underpinned successful initiatives.

- **Favourable regulatory conditions** and experimentation with different approaches were often critical. For instance, public-private partnerships (e.g. the Aashkar tablet in India[7]) were used to support outreach to poorer communities in India or South Africa. In Kenya, the success of M-PESA would not have been possible without regulations enabling this type of service development.

- **Private entrepreneurial initiative** was a driver of scale. Private companies (e.g. Nokia and Motorola) have adapted handsets for the developing world, while MFIs have received a substantial boost from participation by commercial banks. Other actors – notably

Table 1.4. **Pricing and financing strategies**

Strategy	Examples
Pay-as-you go: users pay in small units instead of high fixed costs for service access.	• In India, the **Byrraju Foundation** provides water purification services through community filtration plants at half the price of alternative methods. The business model is pay-per-use. • In Medellin (Colombia), the main electricity provider **EPM** has developed a pay-as-you-go card for customers whose service was cut for reasons of non – payment. This initiative has reconnected these customers to the system.
Tiered pricing: price discrimination whereby higher-income users cross-subsidise lower-income users in exchange for extra services, or through other forms of market segmentation.	• In India, **Ziqitza** operates the 1298 programme, a network of fully equipped advanced and basic life support ambulances. The 1298 business model uses a sliding price scale based on patients' ability to pay, determined by the kind of hospital to which they choose to be taken. Financial sustainability is ensured through cross-subsidisation.
Microleasing: potential customer purchase usage rights rather than ownership of product.	• In India, **SELCO** provides solar power to the rural poor. To offset the high one-off cost of installing a solar panel, it treats it as a service rather than as a product. Solar lights are leased out to customers – e.g. farmers or sellers in rural areas – on a nightly basis.
Chain financing: provides innovations and access to financial solutions.	• **CEMEX Patrimonio Hoy** operates in various countries in Latin America. The programme provides access to construction goods, as well as financing and counselling services, stimulating investments of poor households in the housing sector. • In Colombia, **Pavco Colpozos** promotes efficiency in agricultural production by selling technological solutions for water management to farmers, using flexible payment models. • In Mexico, bakery goods producer **Bimbo** (which has a large distribution network) has entered into a partnership with the MFI **Fincomun**. Fincomun agents avail themselves of transport by Bimbo supply trucks to reach their potential clients, small low-income shop owners. Access to the shop owners' payment history when purchasing Bimbo products serves as a first filter for future credit candidates. Bimbo also benefits, since its consumers have enhanced access to credit and are more likely to pay for its products on time.
Credit, savings and insurance improve the purchasing power of lower-income groups.	• Microfinance is perhaps the most important means of reaching the poor. The successful example of the **Grameen Bank** in Bangladesh has led to its replication in a variety of contexts. Many microfinance experiences around the world testify that this contracting innovation, through the concept of joint liability, changes the behaviour of borrowers, reduces monitoring costs and enforces payment through peer pressure – all of which help make credit more available to the poor. • By indexing insurance to measurable scenarios that cannot be manipulated by customers, monitoring and inspection costs decrease and customised insurance solutions can lower risks for the poor. The **BASIX index-based weather insurance**, which reduces monitoring and farm level inspection to confirm crop losses, is one example of this trend.

Source: OECD (2013).

Table 1.5. **Changing production practices**

Strategy	Examples
No frills: focuses on uses that are truly valuable to the poor.	• **Tata Nano**, the world's cheapest car priced at around USD 2 500 in 2012, is based on various business innovations, the most important of which is the no-frills approach. It is a very simple car with few of the "extras" offered by modern cars.
Deskilling and standardisation: divides processes into simple tasks that can be accomplished by low-skilled workers after some training; uses highly skilled workers only for highly specialised tasks.	• **Narayana Health**, a private corporation located in Bangalore, charges patients USD 1 500 for heart surgery that would cost USD 4 500 on the Indian market and USD 45 000 on the US market. Profits are achieved through internal process innovations: 1) specialisation, based on "deskilling" some processes so they can be performed by low-skilled workers; and 2) identifying the complex processes to be performed by specialists rather than generalists. Training low-skilled workers – mainly women – to perform simple tasks allows integrating the poor into the value chain.
Specialisation: standardises processes to make them easily scalable and traceable.	• **LifeSpring**, a public-private joint venture between Hindustan Latex Ltd and the Acumen Fund (India), is a network of low-cost maternity and children's hospitals for the poor. By specialising in healthcare for mothers and children, LifeSpring uses only a narrow range of drugs, which it purchases in bulk at a lower cost. LifeSpring has also identified 90 standard clinical procedures and protocols that are used for process innovations. Doctors devote their time to the tasks requiring their expertise, while other workers perform less demanding tasks. • The NGO **Gyan Shala** in India provides primary education at low cost by using standardised curricula and lesson plans to exploit economies of scale. The approach has also made it easier to monitor the quality of the education provided.
Soft networks: use community networks and their knowledge (including door-to-door distribution and advertising strategies) to address low demand due to limited access to information.	• **VisionSpring** (USA, India, El Salvador) is a network of women selling low-cost eyeglasses through the Vision Entrepreneur programme. • **Hindustan Unilever** (India), through the Shakty Initiative, trains women to become micro-entrepreneurs by selling personal care products. Consumers benefit through better personal hygiene and illness prevention, while women improve their bargaining positions within their households and communities. • The **Arogya Ghar Clinics** for Mass Care (India) are based on a system of mobile kiosk-based clinics operated by women with a high-school education who deliver door-to-door care. • Under the **Grameen Village Phone initiative**, women in Bangladesh and Uganda sell retail phone services within their villages.
Value chain inclusion: leverages the poor to enhance producers' access to resources and knowledge (contract production, deep procurement and demand-led training).	• **Tata Nano** (India) used different cost-reduction strategies, such as an innovative distribution system of establishing assembly units closer to customers in distant areas. Local production allowed Tata to eliminate one step in the distribution chain, helping to improve its relationship with customers and enhancing its corporate image. • The **Aakash Ganga River** initiative (also in India) has helped 10 000 villagers gain access to clean water by renting rooftops from the poor to collect, channel and sell rainwater. • **Nestle Pakistan** has developed a deep procurement model that collects milk directly from 160 000 small farmers. • **Indupalma** (Colombia) integrates farmers in the supply chain for palm oil production. It helps them become landowners, create associations, buy inputs and machinery, and gain access to credit to improve the overall business process.

Source: OECD (2013).

NGOs, not-for-profit organisations and universities and/or public research institutes – have often contributed adjustments to supply a wider market with a better product. Jaipur Foot, an affordable prosthetic foot (currently sold for USD 45) developed by the NGO **Bhagwan Mahaveer Viklang Sahayata Samiti**, has been widely adopted as a result of product innovations involving various research organisations. Similarly, collaboration with Stanford University led to the development of the Jaipur Knee. Thus, private entrepreneurial initiative has been a driver of scale and a core condition for success.

• **Open access to information infrastructures, including data**, enables the development of innovative goods and services. Therefore, equal and non-discriminatory access can maximise the economic and social value of information infrastructures. However, such access needs to ensure individuals' rights for privacy are preserved. One example is the

Ushahidi platform which allows for geolocating events. Available as open source software, it has been re-deployed at low cost to the disseminate knowledge in agriculture in countries as diverse as Argentina (Agrotestigo, 2012) and Afghanistan (Rotich, 2011).

- Building on **existing infrastructures helped achieve scale** by overcoming obstacles through relying on existing delivery networks for the poor (e.g. using small community-based shops) and existing knowledge sources (e.g. NGOs operating in the field). Fuel from the Fields, a grassroots entrepreneurship initiative that allows producing charcoal from agricultural waste, relies on partner institutions to disseminate the technology and know-how to diverse communities (Paunov and Lavison, 2014).

3.3. Microcredit: A successful inclusive innovation

Microcredit – the granting of small loans rarely amounting to more than a few hundred USD – is an interesting case because unlike other inclusive innovations, it is a more mature product that has undergone substantial experimentation and managed to reach significant scale. According to estimates, about 200 million people worldwide were clients of an MFI in December 2010, of which over 130 million were living in extreme poverty – i.e. on less than USD 1.25 per day, or less than half the national poverty line (Microcredit Summit Campaign, 2012). The microfinance market, estimated at USD 60 billion to USD 100 billion in 2013, caters to about 20% of demand for credit by the poor worldwide (IFC, 2013b). Among the various MFIs, the Grameen model (see Box 1.6) is quite widespread, with the Grameen Bank numbering over 8.37 million members in 2012 (Grameen Bank, 2013).[8] Microfinance is also interesting because it facilitates the uptake of inclusive innovations.

Sustainability

Microfinance has proven to be a viable and sustainable business model. A 2006 survey of 702 MFIs in 83 countries suggests that 84% of all MFI clients were served by profitable MFIs, including for-profits and not-for-profits (Quayes, 2012).[9] Research on 14 Ethiopian MFIs suggests that the largest MFIs have cost efficiency scores on a par with commercial banks (Kebede and Berhanu, 2012). Many MFIs receive additional resources – only circa 23% of MFIs worldwide operate without any subsidies (D'Espallier et al., 2013).

There has been some debate about the profitability and role of MFIs in providing a tool to support the poor and ensure sustainability. "Moderately poor" households, rather than the "very poor", have been among the most active participants (Hashemi and de Montesquiou, 2011, as cited in Ledgerwood et al., 2013; see Ghalib, 2013 for evidence on Pakistan). This is partly related to the low scale of serving the poorest (given the smaller loan size), which hinders the development of sustainable business models. To remedy this, formal financial institutions in particular rely on cross-subsidisation, whereby larger-scale funding for higher-income groups provides the necessary inputs for sustainability. Certain characteristics (such as higher repayment rates among the poor) might also, if well managed, provide better opportunities to provide the poor with sustainable business services (Quayes, 2012; Kumar-Kar, 2011). However, adopting the for-profit model might also increase the cost of raising capital, as it will not allow those businesses to access "soft" loans (e.g. provided by social investment funds) and donations, as well as different tax treatments.[10] Thus, a situation where a small number of MFIs catering to special-needs clients co-exist with profitable larger MFIs might be most inclusive in serving poor clients.

Finally, ensuring sustainability will depend on framework conditions – including interest rate ceilings, the status and corresponding tax treatment of MFIs, and the conditions for operating an MFI (which will determine to what extent non-financial entities are involved). These factors affect the opportunities available to develop sustainable microfinance businesses (Imai et al., 2012; Ahlina et al., 2013). Registering as a formal financial institution allows an MFI to accept and mobilise savings for financing purposes. Similarly, commercialisation can help MFIs raise more capital through the regular financial market, in line with the growth of socially responsible investment. The uptake of microfinancing by various entities has allowed adjusting to a diversity of regional contexts and circumstances. Some entities – e.g. financial co-operatives, NGOs and village banks – operate under regulatory frameworks, but not under the supervision of the national financial authorities. Such arrangements have allowed reaching a wider group of the poor than would have been possible otherwise.

Successful innovations behind microfinance

The success of the microfinance model is based on constant efforts to provide sustainable credit services to geographically scattered and remote poor clients. Unlike higher-income groups, these people often have neither collateral nor a credit history and may even sometimes lack verifiable identities. To avoid moral hazard, MFIs needed to find alternatives to traditional approaches (e.g. collateral-based loans to ensure borrowers do not have incentives to default). Providing low-income groups with access to credit group lending with joint liability has been one critical solution, based on three types of models (Box 1.5).

> **Box 1.5. Group lending innovations behind the success of microfinance**
>
> **Microlending models that have proved most successful include the following:**
>
> - **The solidarity group model:** a small group (generally four or five individuals) takes out a joint loan. The payback instalment is usually short and starts very close to the loan's disbursement. Because they are jointly responsible for timely repayment, the borrowers have incentives to select group members with similar risk profiles. Peer pressure heightens the recovery rate.
>
> - **The Grameen model:** an MFI created in a village caters to 15 to 20 villages. The MFI grants joint-responsibility loans to self-formed groups of about five borrowers (as in the solidarity group model). The loans are issued in waves; the first members get their loans, and then the next – if the first members have repaid their due – and so on. One mechanism to improve repayment is peer pressure within the group.
>
> - **The village banking model** is a community-based credit and savings association. A large group (25 to 50 villagers) takes out a joint loan from an MFI and forms a smaller village committee to allocate smaller loans from this common loan. The role of the MFI is limited to administrative and technical issues. **Women's self-help groups,** comprising up to 15 women under the guidance of an NGO or other public actor, generally operate under this model.
>
> - **The individual model:** after screening within informal networks (community leaders, friends, family), the MFI grants a loan to a single borrower. A bailer is sometimes required to compensate for the lack of collateral. Because this model entails larger costs for the MFI and is plagued by more important information asymmetries, it was originally unpopular.
>
> Source: Guntz (2011).

Another solution has been to provide dynamic incentives – e.g. the promise of larger future loans conditional on timely repayment of the initial smaller loans. Other types of innovations have also helped improve the performance of MFIs, as illustrated by the example of SKS (Box 1.6).

> ### Box 1.6. **SKS in India**
>
> SKS is an MFI providing small loans (ranging from approximately USD 44 to USD 260) to poor rural women. Launched as a not-for-profit in 1998, it became a for-profit company in 2005. It is present in 6 Indian states and had over 5 million members as of 2013. To reach this scale and remain sustainable despite catering to a very segmented market and to the very poor in particular, SKS relied on innovative business practices. Various innovations were introduced to adjust processes to the characteristics of their target customers and keep costs down:
>
> - **As many poor customers are illiterate**, SKS developed a visual system to record applicants' information: instead of filling out a written form, applicants declare their wealth by using dashes on pictograms representing different assets (cattle, etc.). This improves trust and facilitates the registration process.
> - **SKS adapted its operations to client schedules.** All weekly meetings are organised from 7.00 to 9.30 so as not to interfere with women's work in the fields. Similarly, SKS adopted a "door-step banking" model where the loan officer travels from village to village so that the clients do not have to waste valuable time commuting to and from the branch.
> - SKS employs loan officers from the same village as the customers (**65% of the workforce is from the same disadvantaged communities as the clients**). This facilitates interaction with clients, reduces asymmetry, cuts costs and empowers the community.
> - SKS took additional steps, including standardising all of its processes (from organising meetings to training new agents).
> - **SKS developed a custom management system.** The software is easy to use for uneducated people, as well as fast – no more than 30 minutes are needed to record the weekly payment and other required data, allowing its use in areas with limited power. The system automatically transfers all information – relatively fast even on very slow connections – to the central computer in the head office for compilation.
>
> Source: Mohan and Potnis, 2010; www.sksindia.com (accessed in March 2014).

4. Conclusion

Inclusive innovations demonstrate that innovation can effectively improve the welfare of lower-income and excluded groups. New technologies, in particular ICTs, have heightened opportunities to develop inclusive innovations. The private sector's interest in serving the growing middle-income groups in emerging economies in particular offers opportunities for inclusive innovations to successfully reach scale despite the many challenges they face – from the lack of financing and technical expertise for grassroots innovators to limited information about actual consumer needs for pro-inclusive innovators. Policy plays a role in creating a favourable environment for inclusive innovations to develop scale, effectively leveraging market-based creativity to tackle these development challenges more efficiently (as discussed in Chapter 3).

Notes

1. The different levels reflects increased inclusion: 1) the pure intention of serving excluded groups; 2) their use and adoption by excluded groups; 3) which, if it then results in improving livelihoods, will be inclusive from an impact perspective. The higher levels include a more intense development of the poor in 4) processes; 5) structure; and 6) beyond.

2. While grassroots innovation has gained more interest recently, it has some historical antecedents in the "appropriate technology" movement of the 1970s and the Indian People's Science Movement of the 1980s (Smith et al., 2013).

3. Poverty is understood here as the lack of valuable opportunities and liberties (Sen, 1988), which results in different ways of marginalisation.

4. Social value creation is increasingly being considered as a core business strategy in support of profits and competitive advantage (Baumüller et al., forthcoming). This is very different from "corporate social responsibility", which became prominent in the 1960s and 1970s with the rise of multinational enterprises and was largely driven by the need to mitigate tensions between multinationals and society.

5. Regarding the standardised case, it bears noting that some of these innovators' products have effectively become inclusive innovations, not by design but simply by the product cycle dynamics based on which ultimately products become affordable. The most famous example here is mobile phones, which have become a critical tool for other service-based inclusive innovations.

6. Although the initial target was USD 2 000, the car's final retail price was USD 2 600 for the most basic model and USD 4 000 for the better version (with power windows and air conditioning). The car is much more expensive than a scooter and unattainable for the very poor (*businessweek.com*, 2014).

7. The Aashkar tablet is a low-cost tablet developed as part of an initiative by India's Ministry of Human Resource Development. Its aim is to serve as a tool to access tailored e-learning content and applications and replace the computer (notably for programming and robotics) (Ministry of Human Resource Development, 2013).

8. Microfinance also has the potential to positively affect non-monetary aspects of inclusive development, such as quality of life, access to education, child labour and women's status in the household and society. The latter is particularly relevant, as microcredit was first designed as a tool to empower women; in 2010, about 82% of the very poor clients of MFIs were women (Maes and Reed, 2012). See, for example, Angelucci et al. (2014) for a discussion of achievements in that respect.

9. Estimates of MFIs for 2002-04 showed that 57% of all MFIs and 53% of not-for-profit MFIs were profitable (Cull et al., 2009).

10. A study of 346 institutions across 67 countries suggests that compliance with prudential supervision heightens costs for MFIs and leads profit-oriented MFIs to reduce outreach as a way to lower costs (Cull et al., 2009).

References

Adler, R. and M. Uppal (2008), "m-Powering India: Mobile Communications for Inclusive Growth", *Report of the Third Annual Joint Roundtable on Communications Policy*, The Aspen Institute India.

Agrotestigo (2012), "Crowdsourcing in Agriculture in Argentina", Crowdsourcing.org, *www.crowdsourcing.org/document/crowdsourcing-in-agriculture-in-argentina/13023* (accessed 09.12.2014).

Ahlina, C., J. Linb and M. Maioc (2011), "Where Does Microfinance Flourish? Microfinance Institution Performance in Macroeconomic Context", *Journal of Development Economics*, Vol. 95 (2011), pp. 105-120.

Angelucci, M., D. Karlan and J. Zinman (2014), "Microcredit Impacts: Evidence from a Randomized Microcredit Program Placement Experiment by Compartamos Banco", *NBER Working Paper*, No. 19827.

Ashraf, N., D. Karlan and W. Yin (2006), "Tying Odysseus to the Mast: Evidence from a Commitment Savings Product in the Philippines", *Quarterly Journal of Economics*, Vol. 121, No. 2, pp. 635-672.

Baggeley, J. and T. Belawati (eds.) (2010), *Distance Education Technologies in Asia*, IDRC, Sage Publications, India.

Banerjee, A.V. and S. Mullainathan (2010), "The Shape of Temptation: Implications for the Economic Lives of the Poor", *NBER Working Paper*, No. 15973.

Banerjee, A.V. and E. Duflo (2010), "Giving Credit Where It Is Due", *Journal of Economic Perspectives*, Vol. 24, No. 3, pp. 61-80.

Baumüller, H., C. Hausmann and J. von Braun (forthcoming), "Innovative Business Approaches for the Reduction of Extreme Poverty and Marginality", in J. von Braun and F.W. Gatzweiler, *Marginality: Addressing the Nexus of Poverty, Exclusion and Ecology*, Springer, Ch. 20.

CEDLAS and The World Bank (2014), *Socio-Economic Database for Latin America and the Caribbean* (database), http://sedlac.econo.unlp.edu.ar/eng/statistics.php (accessed 19 May 2014).

Cull, R., A. Demirgüç-Kunt and J. Morduch (2009), "Does Regulatory Supervision Curtail Microfinance Profitability and Outreach?", *World Bank Policy Research Working Paper*, No. 4748, http://dx.doi.org/10.1596/1813-9450-4948.

Dalla Pellegrina, L. (2011), "Microfinance and Investment: A Comparison with Bank and Informal Lending", *World Development*, Vol. 39/6, pp. 882-897.

D'Espallier, B., M. Hudon and A. Szafarz (2013), "Unsubsidized Microfinance Institutions", *Economics Letters*, Vol. 120/ 2, pp. 174-76.

Dobrovolny, M. (2014), "Citizen Scientists Pitch New Uses for Paper Microscope", SciDev.Net, www.scidev.net/global/biotechnology/news/citizen-scientists-pitch-new-uses-for-paper-microscope.html.

Duflo, E., M. Kremer and J. Robinson (2011), "Nudging Farmers to Use Fertilizer: Theory and Experiemenal Evidence from Kenya", *American Economic Review*, Vol. 101, No. 6, October.

Field, E., R. Pande, J. Papp and N. Rigol (2013), "Does the Classic Microfinance Model Discourage Entrepreneurship Among the Poor? Experimental Evidence from India", *American Economic Review*, 103/6, pp. 2196-2226.

Foldscope (2014), Foldscope website, www.foldscope.com (accessed June 2014).

Foster, C. and R. Heeks (2013), "Analyzing Policy for Inclusive Business: The Mobile Sector and the Base-of-the-Pyramid Markets in Kenya", *Innovation and Development Journal*, Vol. 3/1, April, pp. 103-119.

Gerdon, S. and C. Reimsbach-Kountaze (forthcoming), "Data-Driven Innovation for Development", *OECD Digital Economy Working Paper Series*, OECD, Paris, forthcoming.

Ghalib, A.K. (2013), "How Effective Is Microfinance in Reaching the Poorest? Empirical Evidence on Programme Outreach in Rural Pakistan", *Journal of Business Economics and Management*, Vol. 14/3, pp. 467-80.

Grameen Bank (2013), *Annual Report 2012*, Grameen Bank.

Guntz, S. (2011), "Sustainability and Profitability of Microfinance Institutions", *Research paper*, Center for Applied International Finance and Development (CAIFD), Georg Simon Ohm University of Applied Sciences, Nuremberg.

Hammond, A.L. et al. (2007), *The Next Four Billion. Market Size and Business Strategy at the Base of the Pyramid*, International Finance Corporation and World Resources Institute.

Heeks, R., M. Amalia, R. Kintu and N. Shah (2013), "Inclusive Innovation: Definition, Conceptualisation and Future Research Priorities", *Development Informatics Working Paper Series*, No. 53, Centre for Development Informatics, Institute for Development Policy and Management, SEED, Manchester.

IFC (2013a), *Access to Credit Among Micro, Small and Medium Enterprises*, IFC Advisory Services, Access to Finance.

IFC (2013b), *IFC and Microfinance*, fact sheet, IFC, October 2013, www.ifc.org/wps/wcm/connect/0cf7a70042429b19845aac0dc33b630b/Fact+Sheet+Microfinance+_October+2013.pdf?MOD=AJPERES.

ILO (2011), *Statistical Update on Employment in the Informal Economy*, ILO Department of Statistics, June 2011, www.ilo.org/public/libdoc//ilo/2011/111B09_241_engl.pdf.

Imai, K.S., R. Gaiha, G. Thapa and S.K. Annim (2012), "Microfinance and Poverty – A Macro Perspective", *World Development*, Vol. 40/8, pp. 1675-1689.

ITU (2014), "Key ICT Indicators for Developed and Developing Countries and the World (Totals and Penetration Rates)", *World Telecommunication/ICT Indicators Database*.

Kebede, H. and W. Berhanu (2013), "How Efficient Are the Ethiopian Microfinance Institutions in Extending Financial Services to the Poor? A Comparison with the Commercial Banks", *Journal of African Economics*, 22/1, pp. 112-135, http://dx.doi.org/10.1093/jae/ejs012.

Kickstart (2014), www.kickstart.org (accessed in June 2014).

Kiva (2014), *www.Kiva.org* (accessed on 7 November 2014).

Kothandaraman, P. and S. Mookerjee (2008), "Healthcare for All: Narayana Hrudayalaya, Bangalore", *Growing Inclusive Markets Case Study*, United Nations Development Programme.

Kubzansky, M., A. Cooper and V. Barbari (2011), *Promise and Progress. Market-Based Solutions to Poverty in Africa*, The Monitor Group.

Kumar Kar, A. (2011), "Microfinance Institutions: A Cross-Country Empirical Investigation of Outreach and Sustainability", *Journal of Small Business & Entrepreneurship*, Vol. 24/3, pp. 427-446.

Ledgerwood, J., J. Earne and C. Nelson (2013), *The New Microfinance Handbook: A Financial Market System Perspective*, World Bank, Washington, DC, http://dx.doi.org/10.1596/978-0-8213-8927-0, License: Creative Commons Attribution CC BY 3.0.

Maes, J.P. and L.R. Reed (2012), *State of the Microcredit Summit Campaign Report 2012*, Microcredit Summit Campaign (MCS), Washington, DC.

Markoff, J. (2014), "Science Tools Anyone Can Afford", *The New York Times*, New York.

Mashelkar, R.A. (2014), "Accelerated Inclusive Growth through Inclusive Innovation", presentation at the OECD-Growth Dialogue Symposium on Innovation and Inclusive Growth, 20 March 2014, Paris, *www.oecd.org/sti/inno/Session_3_Mashelkar_Keynote.pdf*.

McIntosh, C. (2011), "Microfinance and Home Improvement: Using Retrospective Panel Data to Measure Program Effects on Fundamental Events", *World Development*, Vol. 39/6, pp. 922-937.

Melhem, S. and N. Tandon (2009), "Information and Communication Technologies for Women's Socio-Economic Empowerment", *World Bank Group Working Paper Series*.

Ministry of Human Resource Development (2013), *NMEICT – National Mission on Education Through Information and Communication Technology*, Ministry of Human Resource Development, India.

Mohan L. and D. Potnis (2010), "Catalytic Innovation in Microfinance for Inclusive Growth: Insights from SKS Microfinance", *Journal of Asia-Pacific Business*, Vol. 11/3, pp. 218-239.

Narayana Health (2014), Narayana health website, *www.narayanahealth.org* (accessed in July 2014).

OECD (2015a), *All on Board: Making Inclusive Growth Happen*, OECD Publishing, Paris, http://dx.doi.org/10.1787/9789264218512-en.

OECD (2015b), *Data-driven Innovation for Growth and Well-being*, OECD, Paris, forthcoming.

OECD (2014), *Symposium on Innovation and Inclusive Growth: Summary Record*, OECD, Paris, *www.oecd.org/sti/inno/Symposium%2020-21%20March_Summary_Record.pdf*.

OECD (2013), *Innovation and Inclusive Development, Discussion Report*, OECD, Paris.

Paunov, C. and C. Lavison (2014), "How to Scale-Up Inclusive Innovation? Policy Lessons from a Cross-Country Perspective", unpublished manuscript.

Paunov, C. and V. Rollo (2014), "Has the Internet Fostered Inclusive Innovation in the Developing World?", *OECD STI Working Paper Series*, OECD, Paris.

Prabhu, J. (2014), "Scaling Up Inclusive Innovation Activities", presentation given at the OECD – Growth Dialogue Symposium On Innovation And Inclusive Growth on 20 March 2014, Paris, *www.oecd.org/sti/inno/Session_3_Prabhu.pdf*.

Prahalad, C.K. (2005), *The Fortune at the Bottom of the Pyramid. Eradicating Poverty through Profits: Enabling Dignity and Choice through Markets*, Wharton School Publications, Upper Saddle River, NJ.

Prahalad, C.K. and S.L. Hart (2002), "The Fortune at the Bottom of the Pyramid", *Strategy + Business*, No. 6, pp. 54-67.

Protoprint (2014), Protoprint website, *www.protoprint.in* (accessed in October 2014).

Quayes, S. (2012), "Depth of Outreach and Financial Sustainability of Microfinance Institutions", *Applied Economics*, Vol. 44/26, pp. 3421-3433.

Rotich, J. (2011), "A Moment of Discovery and Awe", Ushahidi blog, *www.ushahidi.com/2011/12/14/a-moment-of-discovery-and-awe/*.

Safaricom (2014), Safaricom website, *www.safaricom.co.ke* (accessed in June 2014).

Schneider, F., A. Buehn and C.E. Montenegro (2010), "Shadow Economies All over the World, New Estimates for 162 Countries from 1999 to 2007", *Policy Research Working Paper*, No. 5356, World Bank

Development Research Group Poverty and Inequality Team and Europe and Central Asia Region Development Economics Unit.

Sen, A. (1988), "The Concept of Development", in *Handbook of Development Economics*, H.B. Chenery and T.N. Srinivasan (eds.), Vol. 1, Amsterdam, The Netherlands, North Holland.

SKS Microfinance (2014), SKS India website, *www.sksindia.com* (accessed in March 2014).

Smith, A. (2014), "Scaling-Up Inclusive Innovation: Asking the Right Questions?", contribution to the OECD – Growth Dialogue Symposium on Innovation and Inclusive Growth on 20-21 March 2014, Paris, *www.oecd.org/sti/inno/Session_3_Adrian%20Smith%20(paper).pdf*.

Suárez Franco, C.F. (2010), "EPM: Antioquia Iluminada", *Growing Inclusive Markets Case Study*, No. C109, United Nations Development Programme.

Tarozzi, A. et al. (2011), "Micro-Loans, Insecticide-Treated Nets and Malaria: Evidence from a Randomized Controlled Trial in Orissa (India)", *Economic Research Initiatives at Duke (ERID) Working Paper*, No. 104.

The Economist (2012), "Mobile-Money Services Let Us In", *The Economist Newspaper Ltd.*, 25 August.

Von Hippel, E. (2005), *Democratizing Innovation*, MIT Press, Cambridge (MA).

World Bank (2014a), *Poverty and Inequality Database*, http://databank.worldbank.org/data/views/variableselection/selectvariables.aspx?source=Poverty-and-Inequality-Database (accessed in May 2014).

World Bank (2014b), World Development Indicators (database), http://data.worldbank.org/data-catalog/world-development-indicators (accessed in May 2014).

World Bank (2011), World Bank Global Financial Inclusion Microdata 2011, World Bank, Washington, DC, http://microdata.worldbank.org/index.php/catalog/global-findex/about.

Zhenwei Qiang, C. et al. (2012), *Mobile Applications for the Health Sector*, ICT Sector Unit, World Bank, Washington, DC.

Zhenwei Qiang, C. et al. (2011), *Mobile Applications for Agriculture and Rural Development*, ICT Sector Unit, World Bank, Washington, DC.

Chapter 2

Inclusive innovations in education

> *This chapter provides an overview of inclusive innovations in education, with findings from the OECD Centre for Education Research and Innovation (CERI) survey on the topic. It characterises different types of inclusive innovations in education. It describes the rationales and challenges facing them and discusses examples of successful scaling. Strong not-for-profit funding in this sector, combined with important contributions by local organisations, makes reaching financial sustainability and scale less important in this area than in others.*

Inclusive innovations in education can be particularly valuable, as they allow children and adults from socio-economically disadvantaged backgrounds to gain the knowledge and skills necessary to participate fully in the economy. Higher educational capabilities boost grassroots innovators' capacity to engage in innovation, and help democratise innovation for low-income groups. Despite their relevance, however, not much is known about inclusive innovations in the field of education, and yet it is critical that policy makers be better informed in order to support them. To provide further perspectives, the OECD Centre for Education Research and Innovation (CERI) conducted a survey of 71 programmes – many of which were introduced by non-governmental organisations (NGOs) – operating in 2013-14 in 23 countries.[1] This chapter provides initial insights on the characteristics of inclusive innovations in education. It highlights major differences compared with innovations in other fields, as well as major success factors. In the 2015-16 programme phase on inclusive innovation, the OECD will explore these topics in further depth.

1. Characteristics of inclusive innovations in education

1.1. Definition

The *Oslo Manual* (OECD/Eurostat, 2005) defines innovation as "the implementation of a new or significantly improved product (good or service) or process, a new marketing method, or a new organisational method in business practices, workplace organisation or external relations". In this definition, innovation contains a degree of novelty at the level of the organisation, the market, or the world.

This definition applies widely to the private sector. It also applies to education, with small modifications. Educational organisations (e.g. schools, universities, training centres and educational publishers) introduce: 1) new products and services, e.g. new syllabi, textbooks or educational resources; 2) new processes for delivering their services, e.g. information and communication technologies (ICTs) for e-learning services; 3) new ways of organising their activities, e.g. ICTs to communicate with students and parents; and 4) new marketing techniques, e.g. differential pricing of postgraduate courses.

Inclusive innovations in education can be defined as a new or significantly improved product or process, marketing method, or organisational design providing economically deprived groups with enhanced access to high-quality education and educational resources. Beyond income criteria, the groups – including migrants and minorities – generally excluded from the education system, stem from rural and socially disadvantaged backgrounds. The poor are the main beneficiaries of educational innovations, whose goal is to reduce inequality in access to education. The mechanism to achieve this inclusiveness is innovation, e.g. designing low-cost products (such as tablets and curriculum materials), physical infrastructure innovations, novelties in curriculum design and implementation, new approaches to educational collaboration and networks, and new approaches to student assessment (see Box 2.1. for examples). While primary and secondary education are priorities, further training opportunities for adults can also boost their capacities to participate in economic activities, and should therefore feature among inclusive innovations.

> **Box 2.1. Examples of inclusive innovations in education**
>
> **Affordable Maths Tuition, United Kingdom:** One-on-one student tutoring is administered online for multiple competencies in maths. The tutors are based in India and are available at any time, at a low cost.
>
> **eSchool 360, Nigeria:** Created by Zaccheus Onumba Dibiaezue Memorial Libraries, this holistic e-Learning project aims to supply high-quality, low-cost education to rural Africans. It provides local teachers with technological tools (e.g. tablets and projectors) and a blended curriculum.
>
> **Project Mind, Philippines:** This programme provides distance and informal education services by mobile phone. It monitors students' performance through their answers to multiple-choice maths and science questions sent by short messaging service (SMS) and also administers exams through SMS.
>
> **JOBSTARTER KAUSA, Germany:** Financed by the German government, KAUSA helps young people with a migration background gain better access to training positions in enterprises. At the same time, it assists about 760 000 migrant-led firms in Germany in creating new apprenticeship training positions. The programme aims to strengthen small and medium enterprises (SMEs).
>
> **text2teach, Philippines:** This programme provides fast and timely educational content, including more than 900 multimedia materials in video, picture, text and audio format, through mobile and satellite technologies. It also receives feedback and comments via SMS messaging.
>
> **Text to Change, South Africa:** Using mobile phone technology – specifically interactive and incentive-based SMS messaging – to send and receive information that educates, Text to Change engages and empowers people on issues (such as health care, education and economic development) related to well-being. It also runs campaigns in South America.
>
> **Virtual University of Pakistan (VUP):** This ICT-based university currently offers 17 degree programmes; it uses the national telecommunications infrastructure and delivers lectures asynchronously through satellite broadcast TV channels, with interaction provided over the Internet.
>
> *Source:* Zhen-Wei Qiang et al. (2011) for ProjectMind and text2teach; Baggaley and Belawati (2010) for the VUP; OECD (2014a), *OECD-CERI Survey on Inclusive Innovation in Education* for all others.

1.2. The private and public value of education

While the private sector's attempts at innovation are quantified by profits and growth, education programmes can survive through political or donor support. Education's public good character gives it a special status: since education generates social cohesion and other substantial positive externalities, citizens, governments and philanthropists are more likely to support and finance educational non-profit initiatives – even on a long-term basis. Hence, actors who do not hold purely for-profit perspectives are – more so than for other types of inclusive innovations – important actors of the inclusive innovation ecosystem.

Education is also critical to the economy: inclusiveness and innovations in education are strongly interrelated, since inequality has a negative impact on innovation-based growth. In the presence of market failures – i.e. credit market imperfections – the lack of access to capital can reduce investments in human capital (Galor, 2011): talented individuals who would benefit from further education are excluded, and only those with financial resources receive an education. Moreover, if talented low-income entrepreneurs lack access to financing, promising projects cannot be realised. If production externalities – such as learning-by-doing effects and knowledge spillovers – exist and production is characterised by decreasing returns to individual capital investment, then lowering inequality fosters growth (Bénabou, 1997). Since capital market imperfections are greater in emerging and developing countries, the downsides to inequality are likely to be much more important than in developed countries – and to persist over time.

Finally, as the example of India's Gramodaya Schools illustrates (Box 2.2), education can enable individuals to participate in innovation, ultimately democratising innovation and fostering inclusiveness.

> **Box 2.2. The Gramodaya School: Curriculum innovation for inclusiveness**
>
> The Organisation for Awareness of Integrated Social Security (OASIS) in India identified the mismatch between rural students' interests and the national school curriculum as one of the main reasons students dropped out of school early. The OASIS-run Gramodaya Schools provide an alternative curriculum that is more appropriate to rural contexts. Their aim is to expand the rural population's set of capabilities, thereby fostering inclusiveness. Students can choose from specialisations including "watershed, stop dam building and rain water harvesting", "participatory approach, community development and community forest management" and "self-help group development, co-operatives, microfinance and producer's company". Gramodaya School graduates can follow different career paths, e.g. working as "change agents" with the government and NGOs to facilitate rural development. They can also pursue vocational studies to become technicians or shopkeepers, or even attend higher education institutions to become doctors, teachers or accountants.
>
> Night schools – where children from poor rural families who have to work in the fields during the day have a chance to obtain a primary school education at night – are another example of inclusive innovation, initiated by the Indian NGO Barefoot college as far back as the 1970s. Community groups and the Indian government have set up numerous schools throughout the Indian provinces. To date, up to 700 000 Indian pupils in rural areas have attended night schools, whose curricula are also adapted to local needs.
>
> Source: OECD, (2014a) OECD-CERI Survey on Inclusive Innovation in Education; Barefoot College (www.barefootcollege.org/).

1.3. Context

Individuals from lower socio-economic backgrounds have lower educational attainment and are typically less skilled. Young people aged 20 to 24 show an average gap in educational attainment of almost 5 years between the top and bottom quintiles of the income distribution in the 91 countries covered by the *World Inequality Database on Education* (UNESCO). The gap is 2.5 years between young people from urban and rural backgrounds. Programme for International Student Assessment (PISA) results (Figure 2.1) demonstrates that low-income students fare worse with regard to learning outcomes, including in mathematics.

The quality of school facilities, management and teaching practices is generally unsatisfactory in low-income communities. Education services are part of a set of only partially available services in these contexts that exclude lower-income groups. The range of deficiencies is striking, starting with a lack of teachers: an analysis by the UNESCO Institute for Statistics shows that 5.2 million teachers – including replacement and additional

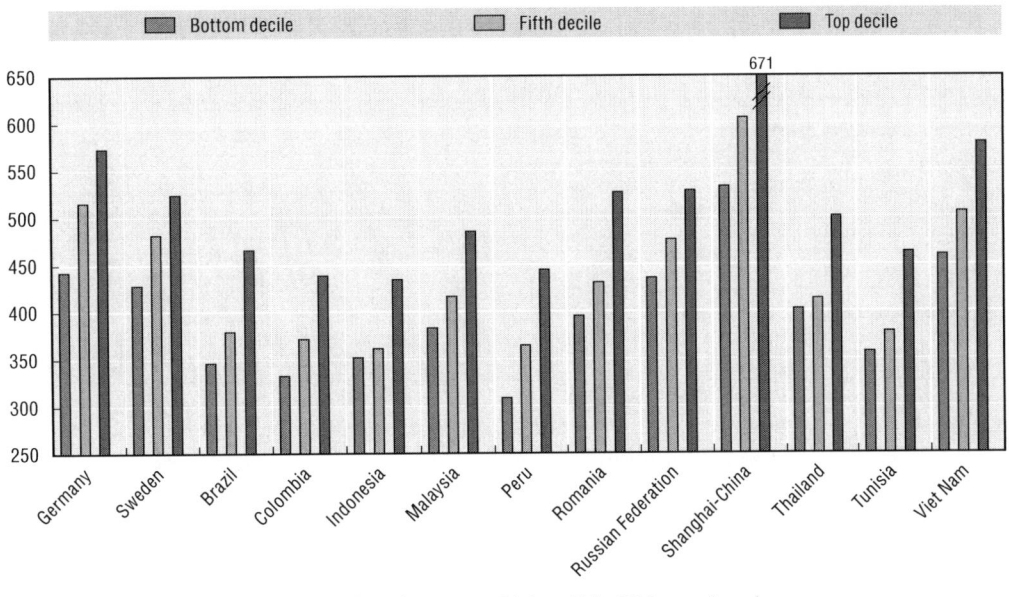

Figure 2.1. **Performance on the mathematics scale, by national deciles of the PISA index of social, economic and cultural status (2012)**

Source: OECD PISA 2012 International Database (OECD, 2014b), http://pisa2012.acer.edu.au/.

teachers – should have been recruited between 2011 and 2015 to ensure universal primary education. This amounts to over 1 million teachers per year, equivalent to about 5% of the current primary school teaching force (UNESCO Education for All [EFA] Global Monitoring Report 2014). Students are more likely to share schools with peers from a similar socio-economic background, reinforcing the potentially negative effects of a lack of resources on low-income students' learning outcomes. Lack of infrastructure – such as inadequate road connections – can compound the challenges and is particularly challenging for underprivileged groups in rural areas. Operations to enhance access to education for these groups generally suffer from incomplete or outdated information on households' socio-economic status, forcing policy makers to draw on indirect methods – such as geographical targeting, community vetting or proxy measures – to estimate household revenues.

Financial constraints are major primary barriers to low-income students obtaining an education in developing countries (UNESCO, 2012). Households are frequently unable to cover the costs of education, from formal school fees to ancillary expenses (e.g. transportation and school materials). In the most extreme circumstances, families face the opportunity cost of children not contributing to household income. Moreover, parents might opt for their children not to pursue their education out of a feeling of uncertainty. They may not have information or knowledge on how to accurately assess the potential return on education due to their own low educational level, or lack of realisation that education should be considered as a long-term investment without immediate benefits (UNESCO, 2013). They may thus perceive the return as too low to justify the costs of education – especially when the quality of the education available to children is low. Social norms within communities may also play a role: parents living in communities where sending children to school is uncommon may find it difficult to object to this "rule" (UNESCO, 2013). Finally, under-investment may also reflect the limited opportunities for lower-income groups to reap the benefits from their investments in the future. The Programme for the International Assessment of Adult Competencies (PIAAC) shows that in OECD countries, the returns on skills are higher for individuals whose parents have attained higher educational levels (Hanushek et al., 2013). This may, however, partly owe to their holding higher "unmeasured" skills.

Another significant challenge is that parent and peer education levels tend to reinforce low overall education levels. In residentially segregated geographies, disadvantaged students are less likely to come across positive role models and mentors who can guide them effectively – and sometimes unconsciously – through the education system and the labour market. Programmes worldwide have sought to reduce school segregation in order to erode the negative peer effects, either through comprehensive desegregation policies or voucher programmes. Other programmes have focused on providing positive role models for students in economically deprived communities.

Low-income communities can also offer opportunities. Their often close-knit nature, centred on a dense network of primary ties, can be extremely valuable in designing and implementing inclusive innovations – much in the same vein as microcredit, which owes much of its success to community cohesion. As a general rule, successful examples of inclusive innovations in education have fully integrated parents – and the wider community – in the process, helping to avoid potential resistance.

2. Scaling up

2.1. How relevant is "scaling up" in education?

Several inclusive innovations in education have been very successful and have scaled substantially. One example is the free and flexible interactive online platform Educarchile, used by 1.35 million students in 2013/14 to prepare for the online national college admission exam. The innovation lies in the fact that low-income and rural students can self-design their curriculum and access the platform offline, as well as on mobile devices. Friends of African Village Libraries (FAVL) is another organisation that has scaled substantially. Since its founding in 2001, FAVL has established and supported 13 small community libraries in Burkina Faso, 3 in Ghana, 1 in Tanzania and 1 in Uganda, reaching 1.15 million people. Its success is based on creating innovative libraries that are more than just a place to read – they have become meeting centres, where community members can gain skills beyond literacy and share resources beyond books. Another example of a successful scale-up is Design for Change, an Indian programme designed to give children an opportunity to express their own ideas for a better world and put them into action (see Box 2.3 for details).

Box 2.3. Design for Change: A successfully scaled project

The Indian designer and educationist Kiran Bir Sethi founded Riverside School in Ahmedabad (India) in 2001 to introduce experiential learning in schools. The programme she designed, "Design for Change", has four steps: 1) "Feel": students observe which situations bother them in their local communities; 2) "Imagine": they interact with the community to identify possible interventions and solutions; 3) "Do": they put those interventions and solutions into action by considering resources, budget and time; and 4) "Share": they share their stories with others to inspire further change. The projects implemented by the school children within their communities range from fixing potholes to stopping child marriages and organising parental literacy campaigns. The simplicity and ease of implementation of the curriculum allowed Design for Change to spread rapidly:

> Box 2.3. **Design for Change: A successfully scaled project** *(cont.)*
>
> the curriculum expanded to other schools in the city of Ahmedabad in 2007 and throughout India starting in 2009 (by 2013, 2 579 schools had participated, involving more than 170 000 students). Since each classroom addresses the problems identified by its students, the curriculum is not context-specific and can be applied worldwide, while still maintaining the programme's core structure. Bir Sethi credits the TED Talk she gave in Mysore in 2009 with helping to spread the idea around the world. Design for Change is currently running in 34 countries; it numbers 160 000 students, 400 000 alumni, 10 000 participating schools and 40 000 participating teachers.
>
> Source: CERI-OECD Survey on Inclusive Innovation in Education (OECD, 2014a); Design for Change website (www.dfcworld.com/), CII-OECD (2014).

Then again, innovations that are positive on a local scale might be undesirable on a larger scale. When exported to new places, such an innovation might no longer be relevant to learners; it may also be unfeasible due to technical constraints, or excessively dependent on a single lead person. Many educational innovations fail because they are not designed for the average practitioner. Teach for India, the Indian social franchise of Teach for All, expressed concerns over its ability to ensure the same level of resources, candidates and professionalism as the project expanded to more schools and states, struggling to maintain the high number of participating teachers required for the process. Learning from its originator, Teach for America, Teach for India streamlined its recruitment, application and selection process to improve scalability.

2.2. Are conditions for successful inclusive innovations in education different?

As discussed in Chapter 1, innovations must overcome a number of challenges. These barriers – meeting the needs of the poor, defining the role and obtaining the support of private businesses, setting regulatory and government conditions, using existing infrastructures and institutions, identifying cost-saving opportunities for sustainability and working within the specific context of the innovation – also hold true for education. As the examples in Box 2.4 demonstrate, one important element of successful scaling is diffusion.

> Box 2.4. **Scaling and diffusion**
>
> **Teach for All: Social franchising**
>
> Teach for All was founded in 2007 "to expand educational opportunity around the world by increasing and accelerating the impact of social enterprises that are cultivating the leadership necessary for change". At the origin of Teach for All is the Teach for America initiative, founded in 1990, which places recent university graduates to teach in low-income community schools for two years. The programme inspired similar initiatives; Teach for All is the global network co-ordinating these programmes. Teach for All uses this modified social franchising model to scale up by sharing branding, support, guidance and resources with its networked social enterprises. The Teach for All network currently comprises 33 national organisations and has reached 5 million students. Teach for All partners with national organisations 12 to 18 months before a programme launch. It offers the founders a three-day immersive training workshop aiming to create social enterprises that are adapted to local contexts and independent from government control, but operated in partnership with

> **Box 2.4. Scaling and diffusion** *(cont.)*
>
> the public and private sectors. Participating organisations also share best practices through peer-to-peer connections, leadership development and conferences.
>
> **BRAC: Horizontal scaling**
>
> BRAC (formerly Bangladesh Rural Advancement Committee) started in 1972 in Bangladesh as a rural rehabilitation organisation, but quickly expanded beyond that purpose. It uses a holistic approach to development to create inclusive projects initiated and controlled by the poor through scalable grassroots solutions to issues in education, healthcare, community empowerment, social enterprise and microfinance. Its microfinance and social enterprise projects bring in the bulk of their operating budget, creating less reliance on donors. BRAC follows a horizontal scaling model to create new, small-scale, holistic projects in communities. BRAC is now the largest NGO and secular private education organisation in the world, with hundreds of thousands of staff and BRAC-trained community members working with over 135 million people in 11 countries in Asia, Africa and the Caribbean and 700 000 students enrolled in its primary schools. The schools bring education to communities that cannot access formal education, focusing on children affected by violence, displacement, discrimination and extreme poverty; they also run mentoring, extracurricular and e-learning programmes. By creating holistic projects in local contexts, BRAC has been able to scale horizontally in a sustainable way.
>
> **Annual Status of Education Report (ASER): Diffusion of innovation**
>
> ASER (which means "impact" in Hindustani) is a national household survey of enrolment, literacy and numeracy conducted throughout rural India by Pratham, an Indian NGO for innovative learning. Each child in the representative sample of 5-16 year-olds is interviewed one-on-one by local volunteers with the support of the ASER Centre and local organisations. ASER aims to spotlight learning issues and provide evidence for policy makers and practitioners. Its success stems from national and international recognition through a critical mass of policy documents, academic research, media reports and international awards; as a result, organisations in Pakistan, Kenya, Tanzania, Uganda, Mali and Senegal have adopted ASER in their national contexts. To support this adaptation, ASER shares best practices of the Indian model through conferences, meetings, trainings and online videos, but does not specifically run the additional assessments. Its founders hope that as more countries use the model, more children will be enrolled in school and learning.
>
> Source: OECD-CERI Survey on Inclusive Innovation in Education (OECD, 2014a); for BRAC: contribution to the CII-OECD Workshop on Innovative Efforts for Universal Quality Education, July 2014; Smillie, I. (2009), *Freedom from Want: The Remarkable Success Story of BRAC, the Global Grassroots Organization That's Winning the Fight Against Poverty*, The University Press Limited, Dhaka, Bangladesh.

Sustainability and scaling up are often confused. Although sustainability can make scaling up easier and scaling up can lead to greater sustainability, sustainability does not automatically lead to greater scale, and an inclusive innovation that grows too large can easily fail. Chapitô's Magical Bag Circus Arts for Social Inclusion in Lisbon (Portugal) shows clear sustainability as the oldest programme in the Inclusive Innovation for Education survey (OECD, 2014a). Magical Bag aims to help marginalised youth develop communication and social skills through workshops focusing on circus, capoeira, music, storytelling and oral tradition. The programme has existed since 1985, but has not scaled beyond the Lisbon neighbourhoods where it was established. Its sustainability comes from Chapitô's status as a major cultural centre in Lisbon, offering performances that attract both locals and tourists. Magical Bag illustrates that sustainable innovations do not need to scale up to be successful.

By the same token, scaling up is sometimes confused with mainstreaming. Mainstreaming seeks to make the innovation the norm in society, while scaling up aims to bring an inclusive innovation to as many people as may need it and use it. The two are nevertheless closely intertwined when large organisations and governments become involved in inclusive innovation in education. While some small NGOs or private organisations that create social-sector innovations prefer to be ignored by government, some seek government support to expand their innovations as they attempt either to mainstream or grow them to scale. By contrast, government agencies that have created or adopted innovations, and large national or multinational NGOs, are generally able to mainstream their ideas faster thanks to their larger network and widespread influence. BRAC, which is responsible for over 1 million students in primary education in Bangladesh, is able to negotiate with the government to mainstream its innovations: the government provides BRAC with textbooks for grades IV and V, while BRAC promises a smooth transition from its primary schools to government-run secondary schools.

Governments that create or adopt innovations also have the ability to mainstream them almost immediately, although the question of selecting those innovations arises. At the recent OECD workshop on "Innovative Efforts for Universal Quality Education", participants suggested mechanisms to select innovations for scaling and mainstreaming. Suggestions included summative evaluations of innovations, randomised control trials and assessments to determine the potential success of given innovations.

Just as scaling up must be carefully considered, mainstreaming an innovation cannot be decided without evidence and appropriate support. First, successful mainstreaming must take into account the original innovation's local context and determine whether is suitable to other contexts or needs to be adapted. Second, educational innovations must find willing participants to grow programmes. Third, while government regulations need not necessarily support inclusive innovation in education, they should not specifically prevent it. Finally, innovators should determine beforehand whether mainstreaming will be sustainable for their organisation, i.e. whether they intend to turn the innovation into accepted practice for society as a whole or whether they should simply focus on selected populations.

2.3. Funding and financial sustainability

When it comes to financing, educational innovations are different from other inclusive innovations. Some education programmes – e.g. private initiatives targeting wealthy households – operate as regular businesses, particularly in countries that do not provide comprehensive, high-quality public education. These for-profit organisations invest in innovative ideas from which they expect long-term financial returns and rely on regular financial channels and models to obtain capital. In most cases, however, innovative educational programmes are developed within the public education system; they may also be private not-for-profit initiatives, funded mainly through public budgets or philanthropic means, or hybrid projects using for-profit models to fund not-for-profit programmes (Foster et al., 2009).

Education is generally considered as a public good generating social cohesion and other substantial positive externalities. This means that citizens, governments and philanthropists are more likely to support and finance educational not-for-profit initiatives, and even to commit to long-term funding. While some for-profit organisations do exist, donations and philanthropy generally play an important role, particularly with regard to inclusive innovations. Thus a better price-performance ratio, while still relevant in education, is not a necessary condition for sustaining and scaling up inclusive innovations. Teach for All (see Box 2.4.), whose national organisations rely mainly on public funding and donations, has successfully scaled up without being constrained by its operations' price-performance ratio. Few projects, however, have considered hybrid models of social entrepreneurship – innovative business solutions to solve societies' most pressing problems – to fund their projects.

That said, cost-saving for wider sustainability is just as important in education. Most programmes rely on volunteers as their main cost-saving strategy;[2] other strategies include making intensive use of existing community facilities (e.g. double-shift schools), ICTs (as with other inclusive innovations) and low-cost materials, as well as focusing on self-instruction. Indeed, some projects have stated that (short-term) efficiency is not a primary goal. Fundación Ventanas, which provides loans to Colombian students who would not otherwise be able to afford higher education, relies on an interesting financing model. With seed money from a wealthy donor, Fundación Ventanas started its first round of loans for high-achieving poor students, who commit to paying off their loans once they find employment by funding future loans for other low-income students. This self-sustaining model funds both future loans and the programme's operations.

Fundación Paraguaya is another social enterprise that successfully developed self-sustaining inclusive education innovations. Founded in 1985 as the first microfinance organisation in Paraguay, Fundación Paraguaya now operates three separate programmes. The microfinance project has been financially self-sufficient since the 1990s. The Entrepreneurial Education Programme teaches entrepreneurship to primary and secondary students in (mainly urban) public and private schools and has been self-sufficient since the late 1990s (Maak & Stoetter, 2012). Finally, the agricultural school was developed in 2002 in partnership with a Catholic agricultural school in financial difficulty. Based on Fundación Paraguaya's entrepreneurial curriculum and microfinance experience, the school teaches rural students specific business skills required for their agricultural experience. The project combines a traditional secondary education with the creation of small, student-run enterprises focusing on sustainable farming. The school uses these enterprises, along with funds from the microfinance programme, to finance itself; it also helps alumni create their own businesses through microfinance loans. Thanks to this model, the school was able to achieve self-sufficiency in 2007 (Baird & Harrelson, 2008).

The social enterprise model is not right for every programme, and innovative projects in education can use their not-for-profit status to garner greater support. A not-for-profit organisation that provides a public good and targets the poorest of the poor also garners more support from community members working as volunteers. This, in turn, can have a tremendous impact on an organisation's finances. Employing 25 000 volunteers for each of its annual surveys in addition to 100 regular employees, ASER would certainly not operate at the same scale without unpaid workers. In the OECD Survey on Inclusive Innovation in Education (OECD, 2014a), half of the programmes had more volunteers than permanent employees and one-third had more volunteers than permanent and temporary employees combined. Thus, having a good strategy to attract volunteers is an important consideration when designing an innovative educational programme targeting cash-strapped households.

2.4. Stakeholder involvement

Innovators need to ensure that teachers, parents and the broader community feel part of the innovation process. Respondents to the OECD survey (OECD, 2014a) often cite a lack of demand as a problem, even when the product or service is free and beneficial to potential consumers or students. Problems may also start as early as finding schools and teachers willing to participate in a particular innovation, as teachers may be unwilling to change from well-known routines to new practices: Xseed Education, a pedagogical innovation emphasising experience, analysis, application and step-by-step lesson plans, initially met with strong resistance from teachers, who admitted they tried to avoid Xseed staff for weeks – even months. The reason for this is that unlike entrepreneurs, teaching staff do not necessarily have incentives to engage in inclusive innovation initiatives.

3. Conclusion

Education is often perceived as the way out of poverty, crime and ignorance for socio-economically disadvantaged groups. Inclusive innovations in education have helped increase access to education for excluded groups, as well as strengthened capacity building for grassroots entrepreneurship. While inclusive innovations in education share many of the characteristics of other inclusive innovations, there are some differences. First, inclusive innovations for education are public goods, and hence require special attention – and funding – from policy makers. Second, the conditions for, and characteristics of, scaling up inclusive education can differ according to the innovation type. Chapter 3 discusses these wider policy implications.

Notes

1. Additional information was obtained from the inventories of the Center for Education Innovations, the World Innovation Summit for Education and the Education Innovation Fund for India. The analysis also benefitted from discussions at the International Conference for Universal Quality Education organised by the OECD, India's Planning Commission and the Confederation of Indian Industry. Individual projects were also contacted by email or phone to qualify their answers to the OECD survey or gather additional information about their innovations. The survey combines closed and open-ended questions to collect detailed information about the projects, including funding sources, goals, size, target groups, type of innovation, community involvement, origin of the innovative idea and unexpected problems or impacts of the innovation.

2. In the world of inclusive innovations, an important aspect to consider is the reward system for volunteers, who tend to represent a significant proportion of the total workforce. In order to retain volunteers, projects use symbolic stipends, offer promotion opportunities, certificates and on-the-job training, or simply make volunteers feel part of a unique learning community.

References

Baird, A. and W. Harrelson (2008), *Analysis of Fundación Paraguaya's Financially Self-Sufficient Agricultural High School: Documenting a Model of a Financially Self-Sustaining School and the Opportunities and Challenges for Replication*, Inter-American Development Bank, Washington, DC.

Bénabou, R. (1997), "Inequality and Growth", *NBER Working Paper*, No. 5658.

Baggeley, J. and T. Belawati (eds.) (2010), *Distance Education Technologies in Asia*, IDRC, Sage Publications, New Dehli.

CII-OECD (2014), *Workshop on Innovative Efforts for Universal Quality Education* (various contributors), New Delhi, July 2014, http://cii-uic.in/en/events/cii-oecd-workshop-july14.

Foster, W., P. Kim and B. Christiansen (2009), "Ten Non-profit Funding Models", *Stanford Social Innovation Review*, Spring, pp. 32-39.

Galor, O. (2011), "Inequality, Human Capital Formation and the Process of Development", *NBER Working Paper*, No. 17058.

Hanushek, E. et al. (2013), "Returns to Skills around the World: Evidence from PIAAC", *NBER Working Papers*, No. 19762.

Kiran Bir Sethi (2009), "Kids, take charge", presentation for TEDIndia filmed on November 2009, www.ted.com/talks/kiran_bir_sethi_teaches_kids_to_take_charge.

Maak, T. and N. Stoetter (2012), "Social Entrepreneurs as Responsible Leaders: "Fundación Paraguaya' and the Case of Martin Burt", *Journal of Business Ethics*, Vol. 111/ 3, pp. 413-430.

OECD (2014a), *Survey on Inclusive Innovation in Education*, OECD-CERI, Paris.

OECD (2014b), *Programme for International Student Assessment (PISA)*, PISA 2012 Database, OECD, Paris, http://pisa2012.acer.edu.au/.

OECD/Eurostat (2005), *Oslo Manual: Guidelines for Collecting and Interpreting Innovation Data, 3rd Edition*, The Measurement of Scientific and Technological Activities, OECD Publishing, Paris, http://dx.doi.org/10.1787/9789264013100-en.

Smillie, I. (2009), *Freedom from Want: The Remarkable Success Story of BRAC, the Global Grassroots Organization That's Winning the Fight Against Poverty*, The University Press Limited, Dhaka.

UNESCO (2014), *World Inequality Database on Education (WIDE)*, UNESCO, www.education-inequalities.org.

UNESCO (2013), *EFA Global Monitoring Report 2013/4*, UNESCO Publishing.

UNESCO (2012), *EFA Global Monitoring Report 2012*, UNESCO Publishing.

Zhen-Wei Qiang, C. et al. (2011), *Mobile Applications for Agriculture and Rural Development*, ICT Sector Unit, World Bank, Washington, DC.

Chapter 3

Policies in support of inclusive innovation

The chapter discusses innovation policy approaches to support inclusive innovation, focusing on policy examples from China, Colombia, India, Indonesia and South Africa. It reviews the rationale for public support for inclusive innovations and outlines the adjustments required for policies to incorporate related obstacles. It then discusses co-operation challenges at the government level and beyond, providing examples of cases where they have been successfully addressed. It follows by examining how policy instruments can support inclusive innovations, notably through opportunities for accessing finance, knowledge and expertise. Finally, it highlights possible ways to improve financial opportunities for inclusive innovation, particularly through regulatory frameworks ensuring consumer safety without hindering private firms from providing health and education services.

The baseline justification for supporting inclusive innovation strategies is that they may alleviate poverty more effectively than other approaches. Indeed, these alternative approaches 1) do not seek "novel" efforts to improve conditions for the poor (i.e. they are not innovation-based); and 2) do not focus on developing business opportunities to serve "poor markets". As inclusive innovations aim to use the market as an instrument to provide key goods and services, they can leverage broader capabilities and tackle poverty in a more cost-efficient manner than other strategies.

However, few initiatives have effectively reached scale. This leaves a large untapped potential, as long as the various obstacles to these innovations are not addressed. Many of the challenges to inclusive innovators – including grassroots innovators – are similar to those faced by "standard" innovators: skills and capacity building are often critical, while financing – and access to knowledge networks – can be difficult. This chapter identifies policy responses that are particularly critical to inclusive innovation, drawing on examples from China, Colombia, India, Indonesia and South Africa to illustrate its arguments. Paunov and Lavison (2014) provide a more extensive discussion, with further policy examples.

The remainder of the chapter is structured as follows: Section 1 discusses the roles of innovation policy in support of inclusive innovation. Section 2 focuses on co-operation challenges. Section 3 reviews the different policy instruments supporting inclusive innovation initiatives. Section 4 concludes.

1. The role of innovation policies in supporting inclusive innovation

1.1. Rationales for public policy support

Governments may wish to consider supportive policies for inclusive innovations for the following three reasons:

- First, inclusive innovations are characterised by various types of market failures – e.g. barriers to information about customer needs, infrastructural challenges such as weak electricity and broadband connections and credit access shortcomings – that make it difficult to supply poor markets. These factors may impose a "poverty penalty" (Mendoza, 2011) – i.e. a higher cost of supplying goods and services to the poor than to higher-income markets – leading to potentially higher prices for such markets, or even "missed markets" when businesses decide not to supply them at all. These combined obstacles can create substantial "sunk costs", which single firms may not be able to address. A limited provision of inclusive innovations may also result from co-ordination failures, wherein government fails to play a critical role in aligning the required actors to address the various challenges.

- Second, many of the products involved in inclusive innovation activities are public services (education, health, transportation, etc.) from which the poor often find themselves excluded. As a critical provider and regulator of these services, the government is automatically a relevant stakeholder in related innovation activities.

- Third, inclusive innovation provides an opportunity to empower lower-income groups and help them move out of poverty, providing an additional rationale for policy action (OECD, 2012a). Much as inclusive innovations serve as pragmatic alternatives to providing services, supporting business activities already performed by the poor (rather than trying to integrate them directly in the formal economy) might constitute a more successful step towards economic development. If such bottom-up innovations also served growth objectives, then there would be an additional rationale justifying their contributions. See Paunov and Guellec (2015) for a discussion of these questions.

1.2. Policy approaches to inclusive innovation

Box 3.1 summarises and defines different national policy approaches to social and inclusive innovations.

> **Box 3.1. Inclusive innovation policy initiatives in China, Colombia, India, Indonesia and South Africa**
>
> **China:** "Inclusive innovation" initiatives in China fall under the headings "science and technology for public wellbeing", "poverty alleviation through science and technology" and "science and technology for rural development" (Chinese Academy of Science and Technology for Development [CASTED], 2014). These initiatives consider how a growing urban population can benefit from these services. "Pro-inclusive" innovations are discussed more particularly in the context of supplying affordable healthcare, education and sanitation. Grassroots initiatives have also been adopted, e.g. in agriculture, with the Science and Technology Demonstration Programmes helping small farmers to modernise their activities thanks to technology.
>
> **Colombia:** Colombia's National Development Plan for 2010-14 aims to "align its economic development to its social development" by providing incentives and removing barriers to social innovation. The country's social innovation policy (the "National Node on Social Innovation") defines social innovation as "the process through which value is created for society through practices, management models, and innovative products or services that satisfy a need, take advantage of an opportunity and resolve a social problem in a more efficient way than the existing solutions, producing a favourable and sustainable change in the system in which they operate". It emphasises the potential for scalability and replicability, which are understood to promote community empowerment. The initiative is a result of intergovernmental co-operation of the National Agency for Overcoming Extreme Poverty, Colombia's National Planning Department and the Administrative Department of Science, Technology and Innovation (Colciencias).
>
> **South Africa:** Policy discussions emphasising the empowerment of excluded populations – where exclusion relates not only to poverty, but also to race, gender and disability – focus on innovation's contributions to inclusive development. "Innovation for inclusive development" can be inclusive both in terms of output/outcomes and the process itself. It encompasses a) pro-inclusive innovations, especially insofar as they develop access to "basic services" (health, education and human settlement), with the involvement of science councils; and b) grassroots innovations, as a way to empower excluded groups and generate employment.
>
> **India:** The term "inclusive innovation" is widely used in India to describe innovations that "solve the problems of citizens at the base of the economic pyramid" (National Innovation Council, 2013). Grassroots innovations also receive strong support from, and

> **Box 3.1. Inclusive innovation policy initiatives in China, Colombia, India, Indonesia and South Africa** *(cont.)*
>
> underpin the activities of, the National Innovation Foundation (NIF), which "provides institutional support to grassroots innovators and traditional knowledge holders from the unorganised sector of the society" (NIF, 2014).
>
> **Indonesia:** Government initiatives dealing with inclusive innovation focus on incremental innovation, with particular emphasis on process innovation. The main governmental actors are ministries, e.g. the Ministry of National Development Planning and the Ministry of Social Affairs, but also non-ministerial governmental institutions, e.g. the National Team for Accelerating Poverty Alleviation. To date, the idea of inclusive innovation has yet to be promoted in the country so that no specific policy to support inclusive innovation currently exists. However, some district governments have started to introduce participatory development planning, which aims to include all communities.
>
> *Source:* For China, Colombia, South Africa and India: OECD, based on comments received from the Advisory Group of the OECD Innovation for Inclusive Growth Project in the Advisory Group meetings on 19 March and 3 July 2014; for Indonesia: Universities and Councils Network for Innovation for Inclusive Development (UNIID-SEA, 2013).

1.3. Obstacles to inclusive innovation and policy implications

By virtue of the characteristics described in Chapters 1 and 2, inclusive innovation requires special policy attention (Figure 3.1). Standard policy measures might not focus as much on consultative processes to fully understand market demand and the role of different actors, and may fail as a result.

Figure 3.1. Obstacles to inclusive innovation and types of possible policy responses

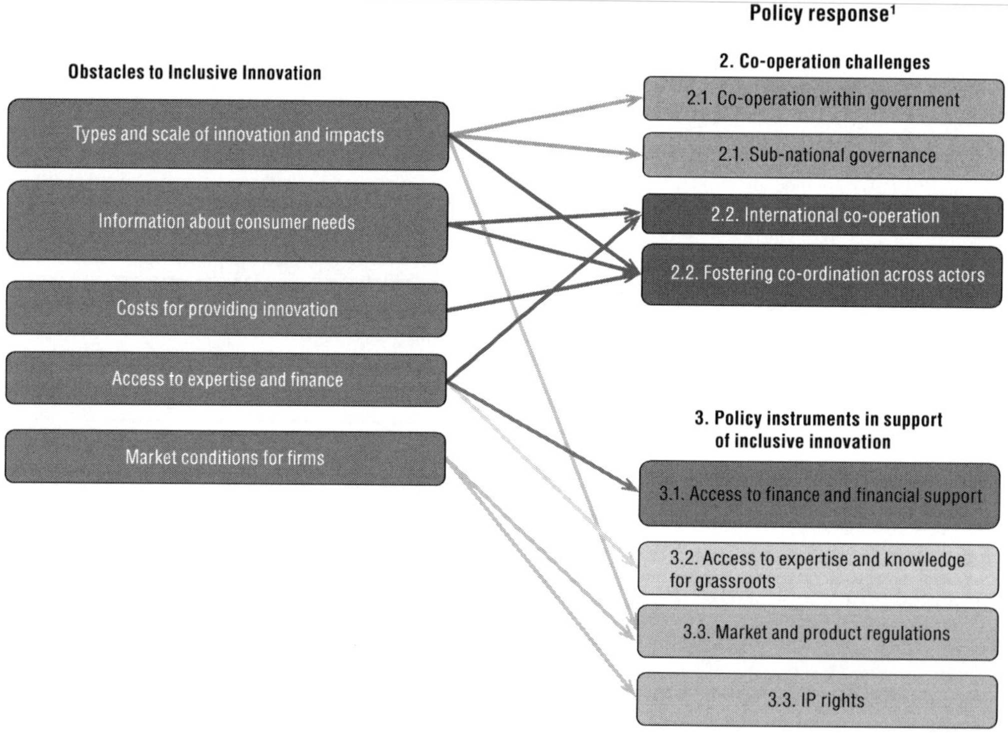

Obstacles to Inclusive Innovation:
- Types and scale of innovation and impacts
- Information about consumer needs
- Costs for providing innovation
- Access to expertise and finance
- Market conditions for firms

Policy response[1]

2. Co-operation challenges
- 2.1. Co-operation within government
- 2.1. Sub-national governance
- 2.2. International co-operation
- 2.2. Fostering co-ordination across actors

3. Policy instruments in support of inclusive innovation
- 3.1. Access to finance and financial support
- 3.2. Access to expertise and knowledge for grassroots
- 3.3. Market and product regulations
- 3.3. IP rights

1. Numbering according to sections in the chapter.

2. Co-operation challenges

2.1. Governmental co-operation

The policy focus on poverty alleviation and the public character of many services require **cross-institutional co-operation**, especially among agencies in charge of poverty alleviation, health, education, infrastructure and innovation. This collaboration is paramount, as policies in one sector can inadvertently impede success in other areas (e.g. regulations in the health sector may prohibit technology-based service provision, which would lower prices). In this light, Colombia has developed its "Policy on Social Innovation" (described in Box 3.1), co-ordinated jointly by Colciencias, the National Planning Commission (DNP) and the National Agency for Overcoming Extreme Poverty (ANSPE). South Africa has also focused on strengthening co-operation among different ministries: the 2005 "Intergovernmental Relation Framework Act 13" promotes and facilitates national intergovernmental co-operation, particularly in service provision and poverty alleviation efforts. Effective mechanisms to ensure cross-institutional co-operation may involve high-level co-ordinating committees overseeing projects at different stages in the development process and jointly shared budgets for project implementation.

The need to **move beyond national-level governance** is even more substantial for inclusive innovation initiatives. First, these innovations explicitly aim to have impacts on the poor, who are located not only in capital cities, but also in remote rural areas; this requires co-operation at the regional – and even local – level to develop appropriate actions and evaluate their impact. Second, effective implementation requires local knowledge, which is often inadequate at the national level. South Africa's Regional Innovation Forums – which include representatives from the private sector, higher education and government – introduce inclusive innovation in local policy agendas by developing provincial innovation programmes in line with the national agenda and helping to implement innovation initiatives (Mkhize, 2014). Providing opportunities for bottom-up local initiatives that seek to implement national policy guidelines is important for effective regional engagement in inclusive innovation projects.

2.2. Co-ordination requirements across actors

The role of government

Chapters 1 and 2 show the critical role several actors play in ensuring the success of inclusive innovations. Figure 3.2 provides an overview of the main institutions. It indicates that inclusive innovations require support not only from well-known players – government, public research institutes (PRIs) and universities, as well as the private sector and financing institutions – but also from excluded and lower-income groups and non-governmental institutions.

Involvement by lower-income and excluded groups

Involving lower-income and excluded groups in the innovation process – and ensuring that their participation is not marginalised – reduces the risk of low product uptake. It also supports ownership by the communities involved, which is often critical to an innovation's success. Colombia's Policy on Social Innovation (Box 3.2) aims to involve a wider community; the Indigenous Knowledge Systems initiative, led by the Department of Science and Technology in South Africa, involves the informal sector in finding solutions based on indigenous knowledge (Mkhize, 2014). Correctly assessing consumer needs is also at the

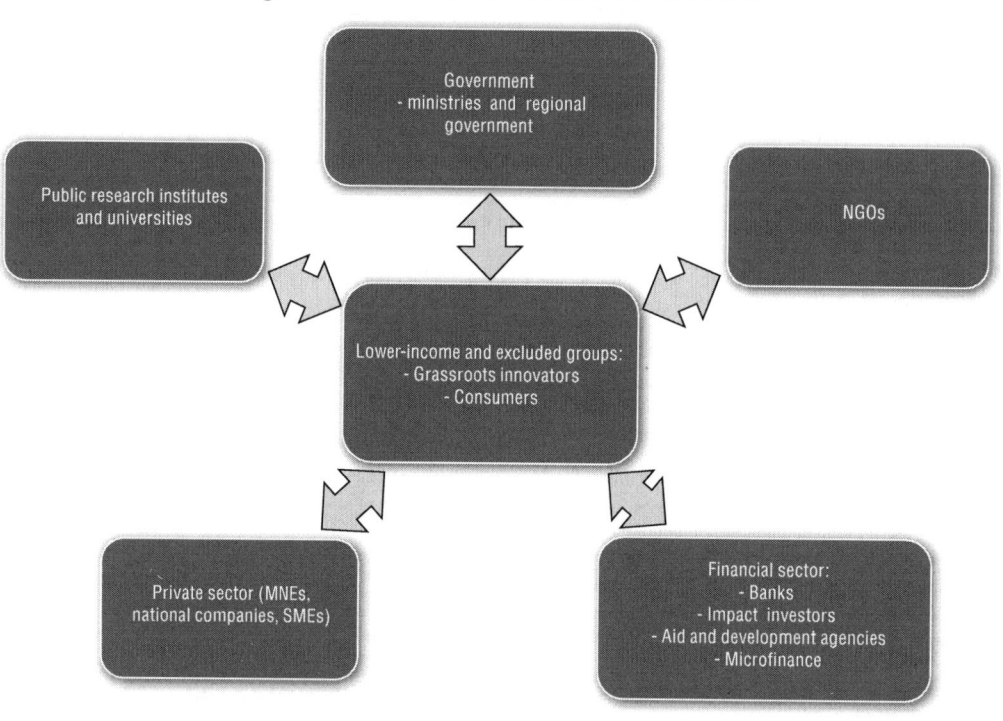

Figure 3.2. **Actors for inclusive innovation**

```
                    Government
              - ministries and regional
                    government
                         ↕
    Public research                         NGOs
     institutes
    and universities  ↘   ↓   ↙
                  Lower-income and excluded groups:
                    - Grassroots innovators
                    - Consumers
                  ↙                    ↘
    Private sector (MNEs,          Financial sector:
    national companies, SMEs)          - Banks
                                    - Impact investors
                               - Aid and development agencies
                                     - Microfinance
```

> **Box 3.2. Colombia's Social Innovation Policy**
>
> Colombia's Social Innovation Policy was developed in line with the country's 2010-2014 National Development Plan. The Plan recognises the central role of innovation not only in the productive sector's development, but also in social and sustainable development and good governance. It also calls for an inclusive innovation system involving all sectors of society.
>
> Several projects have been launched by various institutions in collaboration with the private sector, academia, non-profits, communities, etc. Below are some examples:
>
> ANSPE created the **Centre for Social Innovation (CIS)** in June 2011. The CIS is a co-ordinating body aiming to connect actors from the public and private sectors in order to generate innovative, sustainable and scalable solutions to improve the quality of life of the population living in extreme poverty. The CIS also supports projects through public-private partnerships. It is the only government agency at the national level explicitly using social innovation approaches to develop alternative solutions aiming at extreme poverty eradication in Latin America. Its activities include: mapping the inclusive innovation sector (project HILANDO); public-private partnerships, including calls for inclusive innovation (e.g. "Proyecta Colombia", with Socialab and Ashoka, endowed with a USD 280 000 seed funding prize for each winning project); and partnerships with universities (e.g. academic projects of social innovations, in partnership with the faculties of design of the University of The Andes, Jorge Tadeo Lozano Unviersity and Universidad Pontificia Bolivariana).
>
> In 2012, the CIS launched **Project HILANDO**, which scouts for social innovation initiatives throughout Colombia and records them on an online public directory to facilitate access and contacts among innovators and other actors (*www.hilando.gov.co*).
>
> In collaboration with ANSPE, Colciencias has operated since 2012 another project, "**Ideas Para el Cambio**". Each year, the project selects a priority area (past focuses were the provision

> Box 3.2. **Colombia's Social Innovation Policy** (cont.)
>
> of water and energy access) and consults with communities about their challenges regarding this priority area. It then issues a call for inclusive innovation solutions to the scientific and innovation community based on the results of this consultation. The best ideas for solving the problems receive funds to implement their solutions in the concerned communities. The overall budget is approximately USD 550 000. Project examples include ceramic filters for water sanitation (at the indigenous community of Emberá Chamí in Risaralda) and solar pumps for water provision (at communities in La Guajira).
>
> *Source:* Colciencias (2014); ANSPE (2014a, b, c); Socialab (n.d.).

core of the Inter-American Development Bank (IADB)'s Social Innovation Programme, Innovation Lab and "A World of Solutions" project (Guaipatin, 2014). As Smith (2014) emphasises, scaling up grassroots innovations has its caveats. In particular, it should keep involving communities, since "grassroots innovations are about much more than a product, they relate to various aspects such as community, inclusion, local jobs, reclaiming ownership, etc. Scaling up initiatives carried out by third parties may lose much of the substance of the initial project by overlooking this aspect". A broader policy issue arising is the question of setting up procedures enabling people at the grassroots to contribute to innovation policy agendas (Smith, 2014), since as direct users of inclusive innovations, they have much better knowledge about the challenges facing them. This would reduce information asymmetry for innovators who are not from these groups.

Co-ordination across a wider group of actors

Co-ordination across actors, each fulfilling its own role optimally, is critical to the delivery of public services. Efforts should extend to the poor themselves, as well as to non-governmental organisations, aid and other development agencies, financial institutions, universities, public research institutions and businesses. Experiences in public-private partnerships may help find better means of co-operation. As with the commercialisation of public knowledge, the issue here is not about governmental institutions "taking charge", but about facilitating and supporting private-sector commercialisation efforts (OECD, 2013a). For instance, the public sector does not have the same capacities as businesses and should not venture into commercial activities. Involving business will therefore be critical, with the public sector acting as facilitator rather than actor. Policy measures to serve this objective include, for instance, ensuring regulatory framework conditions that ensure product quality and, consequently, consumer safety but do not at the same time block the private sector from providing services in health, education and transportation at affordable prices.

Many countries are partnering with citizens to innovate in the design and delivery of public services (OECD, 2011a). They do so for several reasons, including a desire to guarantee service quality and cost efficiency. Another rationale or benefit of this process is that it contributes to stronger democracy and trust in government. Both citizens and civil-society organisations may be involved at different stages, from planning, through actual service delivery, to evaluation. Most innovations in public services are incremental, but more radical forms of innovation have been observed in the field of health and social services[1]. Many public services are delivered at a regional or local level, and innovations developed in a particular city or region can also serve as a pilot project for scaling up at the national level. As a result, public service innovations should be promoted at all levels of government. A project in Brazil to improve the water supply illustrates the importance of this citizen engagement in an innovation that resulted in improved services, quality of life and income (Box 3.3).

> **Box 3.3. Improving water supply: The São Francisco Project (Brazil)**
>
> Brazilian governments, public entities, civil-society and private-sector organisations have created a partnership to find solutions to improve water supply in Brazil. The São Francisco Project is a national-level initiative to integrate São Francisco to watersheds in the north-eastern region of Brazil, with the aim of supplying potable water to 12 million people in the states of Pernambuco, Paraíba, Ceará and Rio Grande do Norte by 2025.
>
> Civil-society organisations are involved in the project's social and environmental programmes. They decide jointly on social issues – such as the decision to relocate affected families – and participate jointly in monitoring citizen welfare and satisfaction during and after project execution. The rural population directly affected by the project initially showed resistance to changes; however, the co-production process made it possible to discuss and define their priorities.
>
> As a result, citizens concerned by the project have access to health and education services, sanitation infrastructure and technical assistance to develop irrigated crops on their land. The living conditions of affected families have improved due to relocation. In native communities, actions are taken towards developing craftsmanship to raise the income of families. The effect of the project is a modification of labour structures in the region, permitting the social and economic development of the communities involved.
>
> Source: OECD (2011a), *Together for Better Public Services: Partnering with Citizens and Civil Society*, OECD Public Governance Reviews, OECD Publishing, http://dx.doi.org/10.1787/9789264118843-en, based on information provided by the Ministry of National Integration, Brazil.

Engaging in partnerships to "co-produce" public services aimed at inclusive innovation entails several risks and challenges: 1) government capacities and citizen skills may not always suffice and the cost of services may initially increase; 2) end users may feel that governments do not fulfil their responsibilities to provide certain services directly; 3) promoting innovation by partnering with citizens may counter existing organisational cultures, as it implies that social service providers will be less prescriptive and will give users greater decision-making capabilities; 4) trust in government can be compromised if an innovation fails; 5) the equity and inclusiveness of citizen engagement may be under question if certain population groups end up dominating the process; 6) integrity may be compromised if the service is influenced by fraud; and 7) lack of co-ordination across government levels can lead to conflicting efforts that diminish an innovation's potential effect. In an emerging or developing country context, many of these risks are more acute than in an advanced economy.

Successful implementation and scaling up rely on several factors, many related to the public sector's organisational culture and management (Table 3.1). Effectively managing and evaluating efforts will help select worthwhile innovation initiatives and innovations that require scaling up. The scope of the innovation and the potential rewards for the innovators are other considerations, as the incentive structure in the public sector often

Table 3.1. **Roadmap for successful implementation of partnerships with citizens and community organisations in public service production**

Attitudes and culture	Valuing users and citizens, and openness to their contribution
	Flexibility and willingness to think differently
	Readiness and willingness to experiment
	Creativity to generate a wide range of options
	Cross-organisation perspective
	Preparedness to share skills and devolve power
	Training professionals and users/citizens to develop new skills and attitudes
Systems and processes	Use of a systemic approach – to look at the entirety of service delivery
	Imaginative use of ICT and Web 2.0
	Process improvement – to map existing paths and relationships and scope new options
	Monitoring systems to track impact and evaluate programmes
	More sophisticated budget monitoring systems
Collaboration and partnerships	Citizen and user input at all stages
	The involvement of the private or voluntary sectors
	Empowerment of communities, citizens, or staff
	New skills and ways of working
Management and leadership	Leadership support from the top and at the community level
	Increased rewards to innovative individuals
	Risk management – to identify the risks associated with experimentation
	Evaluation of pilots, and scaling-up of successful efforts
Learning and communication	Looking outward to learn from and benchmark with others
	Using pilots and evaluating what has worked and what has not
	Piloting and diffusion – to spread successful practices
Resources	Seed core resources for innovations
	Bring in resources from citizens, communities and other organisations
	Draw ideas from people at all levels of the organisation

Source: OECD (2011a), *Together for Better Public Services: Partnering with Citizens and Civil Society*, OECD Public Governance Reviews, OECD Publishing, http://dx.doi.org/10.1787/9789264118843-en.

works against innovation. Communities, citizens and public sector staff need to be empowered to engage in public service innovation – whether the service is provided directly by the public sector or through public-private partnerships.

International co-operation

A different and additional level of governance concerns external institutions, which are equally implicated in inclusive innovation and have a longstanding history of involvement in international development work. International co-operation ensures that governments adopt best-policy approaches in this emerging policy domain, learn from existing policy experiences and co-operate with global initiatives (OECD, 2011b, 2007). For instance, the Donor Committee for Enterprise Development (DCED) put together a comprehensive list of bilateral and multilateral organisations that help inclusive business innovators identify partners that may provide them with technical assistance, as well as offer grants and other forms of financial support. The DCED is a forum of approximately 24 bilateral and multilateral donor agencies and private foundations whose aim is to promote private-sector development.

One policy supporting inclusive innovation at the national level is the World Bank's Viet Nam initiative. Endowed with a USD 55 million budget, the Viet Nam Inclusive Innovation Project (2013-18) fosters the development and adoption of inclusive innovations – including grassroots innovations – that tackle development challenges; it supports scaling up and commercialising inclusive innovations through development grants. Key sectors for inclusive innovation include traditional herbal medicine, ICTs and agricultural technologies. Both the Indian Council of Scientific and Industrial Research (CSIR) and the Global Research

Alliance (GRA) provided expertise to support the project's implementation (World Bank, 2014a, 2014b; Mashelkar, 2014). The GRA has also actively supported peer learning and inclusive innovations at an international level (Box 3.4).

> **Box 3.4. The GRA: An international approach to inclusive innovation**
>
> The GRA is an international network of nine research organisations – Battelle (USA), CSIR (India), the Council for Scientific and Industrial Research (South Africa), the Commonwealth Scientific and Industrial Research Organisation (Australia), the Danish Technological Institute (Denmark), Fraunhofer Society (Germany), SIRIM Berhad (Malaysia), TNO (The Netherlands) and VTT Technical Research Centre of Finland – created to "improve the livelihood of the world's poorest through science and technology". Inclusive innovations are a central theme of the GRA, which implements them through partnership-based projects involving end users, local stakeholders and the private sector. The GRA promotes a holistic approach to inclusive innovation, focusing on priorities such as water, health, energy, food security and ICTs and on supporting poor communities in Africa, South Asia and Southeast Asia.
>
> The GRA is currently working on developing a green, low-cost wireless communication network for Africa in partnership with four member institutions – each contributing a specific area of technical expertise to the project – as well as an external organisation locally established in Zambia.
>
> Source: National Innovation Council of India (2013); Bound and Thornton (2012); GRA (2014) www.theglobalresearchalliance.org (accessed 5 June 2014); GRA (n.d.); GRA (2012).

3. Policy instruments supporting inclusive innovation

3.1. Financing for inclusive innovators

Financing is an obstacle for all innovators and has therefore received substantial policy attention (OECD, 2014a). Obtaining financial resources, particularly in the initial stages, can be challenging and often requires alternative financing mechanisms (OECD, 2012b). Inclusive innovators may face steeper difficulties: for reasons explained in Chapter 4, reaching a sustainable scale quickly is more arduous and grassroots innovators are often not well placed to receive financing. Specific funding for inclusive businesses – including inclusive innovations – is particularly weak for the early stages of product development. In India, for instance, most impact funds focus on later-stage financing (Deutsche Gesellschaft für Internationale Zusammenarbeit [GIZ], 2013). Some analysts argue that financial constraints for the inclusive business ecosystem have persisted, despite the considerable growth of the "impact investing" industry in recent years (Koh et al., 2012).

In order to improve financial opportunities for inclusive innovation, India aims to launch the India Inclusive Innovation Fund, a for-profit investment fund that would support enterprises and innovators that provide technologies and solutions aiming to improve the welfare of India's lowest-income groups. Colombia is also planning to launch a special fund for social entrepreneurship as part of a comprehensive support package for inclusive innovators including co-ordination and training services, while South Africa plans to introduce an "Inclusive Innovation Fund". China does not have a specific fund related to inclusive innovations, but the "special fund" dedicated to its S&T Programme for Public Wellbeing has supported 23 projects, including inclusive innovations in health, ecology and public safety (Department of International Cooperation, Ministry of Science and Technology, 2013; CASTED, 2013). Moreover, several regional and local initiatives aim to provide incentives for grassroots innovators: in the city of Dalian, the Municipal Women's Federation operates a "women's online fund" to provide loans supporting entrepreneurship by women who have been laid off, while the municipal government of the city of Nanjing has set up centres providing loan guarantees for microfinance ventures by entrepreneurs.

Financial incentives can also take the form of feed-in tariffs, reduced interest credit, differential taxes for businesses serving the poor and special interest rates for end consumers (Krämer and Herrndorf, 2012). Public-private partnerships are another way for governments to support the development of frugal innovations. South Africa used public-private partnerships at the national and subnational levels to foster inclusive innovation in the water sector (see Amanz'Abantu, a water company that developed an innovative business model to bring water to underserved communities, discussed in Paunov and Lavison, 2014) as well as waste management (see the case of Tedcor, a waste management company that develops entrepreneurship opportunities for informal workers, discussed in Paunov and Lavison, 2014). The Indian government supported the distribution of the Aakash tablet (a low-cost touch tablet that serves as a vehicle for teaching materials and an alternative to computers for disadvantaged students) in 25 000 colleges and 400 universities through public procurement, with a 50% subsidy for a USD 35 subsidised price (Krishna, 2014).

3.2. Access to knowledge and expertise

Providing access to knowledge and technical expertise can be particularly helpful to grassroots innovations. One way to achieve this is for governments to provide incentives for universities and PRIs to support grassroots innovators (Box 3.6). Another is to foster intermediary institutions that build bridges between formal innovation facilities (PRIs, universities) and people at the grassroots level, between innovators and private-sector companies (for scaling up purposes), and between grassroots innovators themselves. The NIF and Honey Bee Network (India) are examples of intermediate institutions (Box 3.5). As

---

Box 3.5. India's National Innovation Foundation and Honey Bee Network

Developed in co-operation with the Honey Bee Network, India's **NIF** creates a link between grassroots innovators and actors who help develop their inventions at different stages. Working closely with the Grassroots Innovations Augmentation Network – which provides incubation and commercialisation support to grassroots innovators from the Honey Bee Network – the NIF operates the Value Addition and Research and Development programme, which connects selected grassroots innovations that could benefit from teaming with the formal research sector (public and private-sector R&D institutions, academic institutions, etc.) to optimise product development. The NIF also promotes inventions in need of development support in an online directory searchable by interested companies. Through a catalogue of innovations, the NIF also allows potential licensers to learn about technologies.

The **Honey Bee Network**, founded in the 1980s by Professor Anil Gupta, is a not-for-profit organisation that documents, supports and circulates grassroots innovations. It manages a freely accessible database of grassroots innovation and traditional knowledge recording over 181 000 ideas. The types of innovations recorded include a) process innovations, especially in agriculture; b) innovative products; c) knowledge on herbal medicine and other community practices related to health; and d) other forms of traditional knowledge (including ancient local agricultural practices). One way to scout for innovations and spread

> **Box 3.5. India's National Innovation Foundation and Honey Bee Network** (cont.)
>
> awareness around them is through the "Shodh Yatras" (journeys of exploration), where volunteers tour remote villages during 100-200 kilometre walks. Participants come from various backgrounds, including grassroots innovators, scientists and students. The Honey Bee Network also supports the development of local networks of farmers, "Shodh Sankal", which share experiences and inventive solutions to local problems. Finally, the Honey Bee Network's Techpedia Initiative mobilises technological students and universities to work on solutions with people at the grassroots.
>
> Similar initiatives inspired by the Honey Bee Network include the China Innovation Network, established in 2011 in collaboration with the Honey Bee Network and the Tianjin University of Finance and Economics.
>
> *Source:* Society for Research and Initiatives for Sustainable Technologies and Institutions (2014), *www.sristi.org*; Grassroots Innovation Augmentation Network (2014), *http://west.gian.org*; Gupta (2012); National Innovation Foundation (2014) *www.nif.org.in*.

> **Box 3.6. The Massachusetts Institute of Technology (MIT) D-Lab**
>
> Spurred by the aim of building a global network of innovators to tackle global poverty, the MIT D-Lab produces pro-inclusive innovations. It brings together students and graduates with science, engineering and business backgrounds to mobilise their skills to tackle development challenges, and offers practical classes on innovation for the poor. D-Lab partners with communities in a dozen countries in Africa, Asia and Latin America that are involved in product development of innovations by students and researchers (e.g. Leveraged Freedom Chair[*], a wheelchair adapted to uneven grounds). Some of its projects have reached international scale (e.g. Fuel from the Fields/Harvest Fuel initiative[*]). D-Lab is also involved in fostering grassroots innovation through its Creative Capacity Building programme (providing training and support to local innovation centres in developing countries) and fellowship programme (supporting scaling up innovations). In addition, it leads the International Development Innovators Network (comprising over 200 innovators in 20 countries). Finally, it is developing an evaluation framework for inclusive innovations, the Comprehensive Initiative for Technology Evaluation.
>
> [*] Paunov and Lavison (2014) provide more information about these examples.
> *Source:* *http://d-lab.mit.edu* (accessed on 23 April 2014).

early as 1986, the Chinese Ministry of Science and Technology initiated the Spark programme, which aims to transfer and diffuse science and technology over China's vast rural areas through grant funds, technology training for farmers and the use of research institutes' know-how to solve local technology problems. South Africa, for its part, has developed a programme that fosters partnerships between universities and communities to innovate for development. Another important way to provide access to expertise is by continuing to improve grassroots innovators' capacities by providing them with training opportunities. Raising educational levels will create more opportunities for lower-income groups to contribute to, and benefit from, more complex innovations.

Networks can ensure joint action – which may be particularly important and helpful for overcoming a variety of challenges – for example by using a common platform to deliver mobile services in health, education, etc. In many cases, inclusive innovators do not simply join an existing market – they create one. This means that they often need to make up for the missing physical and legal market infrastructures. Policy must therefore set specific priorities and align different interests in order to create common networks and platforms. The Colombian Project HILANDO (Box 3.2) is one such network.

3.3. Regulatory frameworks

Market and product regulations

Regulatory frameworks are an important condition for innovation. As stressed in the *OECD Economic Outlook 2014*, strengthening competition would effectively help stimulate innovation and improve resource allocation in many economies. Emerging economies would benefit from lower barriers to trade and reduced administrative burdens on firms, while the liberalisation of services is a common priority for advanced economies (OECD, 2014b).

Informal and grassroots entrepreneurs notably differ in the extent to which regulation is able to ensure they can operate on a "level playing field" compared to other innovators. This is a complex topic, if only because very little is known about informal businesses. The multiple challenges to support small business growth also apply to scaling up inclusive businesses. Regulatory barriers hindering the bridging from the informal to the formal sector have proven particularly challenging (Kubzansky et al., 2011).

Governments have adopted different policies in response to these challenges. In 1999, India's National Commission on Labour formulated umbrella legislation for the informal sector aiming to improve basic labour rights (i.e. health and wage payments) in the informal sector; in 2006, it added provisions to raise worker productivity (through skills development, infrastructure and access to finance). South Africa has implemented policy initiatives to improve business opportunities for informal-sector traders and hawkers in Durban and Johannesburg. Grassroots innovation and the development of ICTs can be a relevant stepping stone for integrating actors in the formal economy (OECD, 2009a).

Product regulation matters across a variety of markets (OECD, 2010). Setting regulations to foster the emergence of new technologies can have far-reaching economic consequences. The effects and timing of regulations are also difficult to determine *ex ante*. Regardless of the impetus for regulation (e.g. competition, environment, consumer protection and health), effectively achieving innovation will require both an alignment of implementing agencies' goals and co-ordination among regulators and the different stakeholders (OECD, 2011c). Regulatory frameworks need to be stable and secure, and yet they also need to provide the necessary flexibility for innovation and experimentation to take place (United Nations Global Compact and DCED, 2012).

Moreover, anticompetitive or unnecessary product market regulation can significantly impede effective innovation. Empirical OECD work has found a negative correlation across national economies between the level of anticompetitive product market regulation and innovation (Jaumotte and Pain, 2005). Of the many policy levers studied, reducing anticompetitive regulation was the second most powerful incentive to raise the level of business R&D spending. More-competitive market conditions had a substantially stronger effect on this measure of innovation than greater protection of intellectual property rights (IPR) or state subsidies for private R&D (OECD, 2013b).

Standards and stable regulation can help create a sound playing field. However, they should not be constraining and should avoid placing a heavy burden on businesses in the scaling-up phase. Standardisation is not always easy to use as a policy instrument. Setting standards is mainly the responsibility of industry bodies and not-for-profit technical organisations; procedures can be slow and bureaucratic, and influenced by large players. This also raises the issue of timing: if standardisation occurs too early, it may shut out better technologies; if it occurs too late, the costs of transitioning to the new standard may prevent diffusion. Another limit on the role of governments in standards-setting is that for many technologies, standards are set openly at the international level. Therefore, efforts to impose national standards through public procurement (for example) are risky and costly owing to technology lock-in and the difficulty of determining the dominant standard *ex ante*, given the rapid rate of technological change and global market dynamics (OECD, 2011c). Setting standards adequately is critical to enabling more-inclusive ICT-based innovations (e.g. cloud computing) (OECD, 2013c).

Intellectual property rights

Intellectual property (IP) rights can play a critical role in facilitating and supporting the activities of informal and traditional sectors (OECD, 2009b, 2014c). However, IP rights are rarely used in the informal economy, where innovators tend to use semi-formal means (secrecy, publishing, non-competition clauses, non-disclosure agreements, contracts and others) or informal methods (lead time, complexity of design or technology, after-sales and services, and customer loyalty) to appropriate their innovation (World Intellectual Property Organization [WIPO], 2013).

Several policy initiatives aim to bring about change in the use of IP rights in the informal economy. Launched in 1998, India's Promoting Innovations in Individuals, Start-ups and MSMEs (PRISM) scheme (formerly known as Techno-Entrepreneur Promotion Programme) aims to foster innovation in science and technology for independent innovators and firms, including in rural contexts and informal settings. Selected innovators receive financial support to develop prototypes and scale up inclusive innovations (ERAWATCH, 2013). IP rights are also a critical element of the support policies provided by the Honey Bee Network and NIF (see Box 3.5).

3.4. Additional policy approaches
Prizes and competitions

Prizes and related instruments can be a particularly effective means of drawing attention to inclusive innovation initiatives. The G20 Challenge on Inclusive Business Innovation aims to identify "business with innovative, scalable, replicable and commercially viable ways of reaching low-income people in developing countries". This global competition received 167 applications between November 2011 and February 2012 – 50% from the agricultural sector and the remainder from the retail, housing, health and education sectors. The OECD Development Assistance Committee has also launched a prize to promote the scaling up of innovations addressing important development gaps.[2] An India-European Union Prize for Affordable and Inclusive Innovation is currently being developed as a collaborative effort between the Indian National Innovation Council, the Indian Science and Technology Department and the EU delegation. The prize would support the development (incubation or scaling up, depending on maturity) of inclusive innovations resulting from collaboration between Indian and European individuals or organisations (National Innovation Council, 2013).

Capacity-building efforts

Capacity constraints – particularly the availability of relevant skills – hinder the expansion of grassroots innovations. As user-led innovations in advanced economies have shown, skills allow for more impactful engagement in innovation activities. Education can also support the adoption of products that do not offer immediate benefits (e.g. vaccines can help address health challenges in the future, but lower-income groups might not adopt them unless they are informed about the benefits). Foster and Heeks (forthcoming) provide several policy recommendations to improve the absorptive capacity of low-income groups. They state that capacity building in the informal sector should be part of technology upgrading programmes and that local informal innovators' creative capacities should be bolstered, e.g. through rural cluster support. Indonesia's National Community Empowerment Program (PNPM Mandiri) is an example of a government-initiated programme designed to empower communities and alleviate poverty. The government provides communities with block grants for spending on projects (related to infrastructure, education, etc.) developed "through a participatory, bottom-up planning process that is facilitated by social and technical specialists who provide advice to communities but do not control the funds" (UNIID-SEA, 2013).

3.5. Definitions and systematic evaluation

As in many other areas, innovation policy requires adequate evaluation mechanisms. This holds even truer for inclusive innovation, which is often still experimental and can benefit from a more active system of "trial and error" in policy making. OECD and World Bank (2014) emphasises that a more appropriate novel approach to innovation policy involves research, experimentation, monitoring, learning and adaptation, all of which need to occur in a context of international openness to knowledge, trade, investment and competition. This new approach also rests on close co-operation with private and non-governmental actors, who are often better placed than governments to identify barriers to innovation and point to areas for productive investment or policy action. Evaluation mechanisms also have wide implications on how policy makers learn from experience; what mistakes are made; how to encourage more entrepreneurial experimentation and appropriate risk-taking (not only by enterprises, but also in policy making); how to openly discuss and build upon both successes and failures; and how to organise, embed and institutionalise such learning in the policy-making process. The mechanisms are critical to a better understanding of the way in which policy can influence the behaviour of (increasingly) complex systems to achieve more sustainable growth and shared prosperity.

Proper assessment requires clear definitions of inclusive innovation and public support policies for such innovation, since these concepts are subject to interpretation and often overlap with other innovation and welfare issues. It also requires evaluations, which need to focus on the impacts on lower-income groups. This creates challenges in that a) an innovation's impact ultimately depends on reaching lower-income groups; b) evaluating the impact of non-technical innovations is often more difficult than for technical innovations (where measures of R&D spending or patent statistics may provide some insights, although these indicators themselves are also subject to criticism); and c) the costs of evaluation can be an obstacle, particularly for small-scale projects with limited resources.

While assessments mostly aim to satisfy donors and decision makers (i.e. by ensuring external accountability), they should be part of a broader strategy to improve programme performance through feedback, workshops, innovator platforms and appraisal of stakeholder reactions, developed iteratively. Such learning should benefit from early and periodic sharing of lessons from policy experimentation at the global level. This entails strengthened mechanisms to identify and diffuse good practices, including through specific knowledge platforms and networks. Policy makers should incorporate monitoring and evaluation early in the design stage to improve the quality and efficiency of public expenditures supporting innovation policy. Box 3.7 provides an example of an evaluation-based initiative.

> **Box 3.7. Education Endowment Foundation (EEF)**
>
> The EEF evaluates and awards grants to organisations that seek to close the achievement gap for low-income students in the United Kingdom. The Foundation started its activities in 2011 with a GBP 125 million (British pounds) grant from the UK Department for Education. It partners with organisations and schools to identify, evaluate and share innovations in education that show evidence of improving success for disadvantaged students.
>
> Examples of projects that have been built based on evaluations are the following:
>
> - "Affordable Maths Tuition", a partnership with Third Space Learning, evaluates the effectiveness of providing one-on-one online tutoring to students.
> - "Challenge the Gap" has created "Learning Threes", where schools partner to share best practices in improving learning for disadvantaged students. Staff from schools meet regularly with facilitators to address issues of leadership, quality and student support.
> - "Parenting Academies" offer training sessions to parents of disadvantaged youth where they learn skills to help their children with literacy, numeracy and science.
>
> Source: http://educationendowmentfoundation.org.uk/ (last accessed on 18 November 2014).

Data collection and evaluation is a central preoccupation of countries implementing an inclusive innovation agenda. Colombia, South Africa and Indonesia have undertaken efforts to map the inclusive innovation system and/or the context for inclusive innovation. For instance, in 2013 the DNP undertook a study on "Barriers and Incentives for Social Innovation in Colombia" to determine which actions and policy instruments the country could develop to create a favourable ecosystem for social innovation (OECD, 2013d).

Two options exist with regard to existing data sources. One option is to investigate firm-level surveys to understand the nature of innovations – which is a challenging exercise, as it is often not a focus, even with surveys tracking the informal economy.[3] Another is to study household data – which can better capture information on informal activities, but often holds little insight on the various dimensions of innovation.

4. Conclusion

Governments can approach the topic of inclusive innovation through multiple critical channels. Co-operation across ministries and different levels in the government hierarchy, as well as creating links between different actors and the poor, are key success factors. Financing mechanisms, adequate regulations and platforms for inclusive innovators, as well as prizes to incentivise such efforts, are effective policy instruments. Evaluations and large-scale assessments also help improve policy and learn from past experience – which requires measuring the impact of inclusive innovations. Finally, inclusive innovation policies need to be firmly inserted in the overall innovation policy agenda, thereby ensuring the joint objective of achieving growth and inclusiveness.

Notes

1. Per responses to the OECD survey on "Innovation in Public Services: Working Together with Citizens for Better Outcomes". There were 22 OECD country and 4 non-OECD country respondents.

2. www.oecd.org/dac/dacprize.htm.

3. The *World Bank Enterprise Surveys* survey not only formal-sector firms, but also the informal economy; they help gather information on an important segment of innovators when it comes to inclusive innovation.

References

ANSPE (2014a), "Centre for Social Innovation", presentation given on 6 March 2014, *www.slideshare.net/ centrodeinnovacionsocial/presentacin-centro-de-innovacin-social-anspe-ingls*.

ANSPE (2014b), Agency for Overcoming Extreme Poverty, Centre for Social Innovation website, *www.anspe.gov.co/es/programa/que-es-el-centro-innovacion-social* (accessed on 28 May 2014).

ANSPE (2014c), Project Hilando website, *www.hilando.gov.co* (accessed on 28 May 2014).

Bound, K. and I. Thornton (2012), *Our frugal future: Lessons from India's innovation system*, Nesta, London.

CASTED (2014), *China's Report on Inclusive Innovation*, Chinese Academy of Science and Technology for Development, Beijing.

Colciencias (2014), Ideas para el Cambio website, *www.ideasparaelcambio.gov.co/* (accessed on 21 May 2014).

Department of International Cooperation, Ministry of Science and Technology (2013), *China Science and Technology Newsletter* No. 3, 10 February 2013, Ministry of Science and Technology, People's Republic of China.

Education Endowment Foundation (2014), website, *http://educationendowmentfoundation.org.uk* (last accessed on 18 November 2014).

ERAWATCH (2013), "Support Measure: Promoting Innovations in Individuals, Start-ups and MSMEs (PRISM)", *http://erawatch.jrc.ec.europa.eu/erawatch/opencms/information/country_pages/in/support measure/support_0011?tab=template*.

Foster, C. and R. Heeks (forthcoming), "Policies to Support Inclusive Innovation", *Working Paper*, Centre for Development Informatics, University of Manchester.

Grassroots Innovation Augmentation Network – GIAN (2014), *http://west.gian.org*, accessed in June 2014.

GIZ (2013), *Shifting the Paradigm, Mapping the Inclusive Innovation Ecosystem for MSME*, GIZ, Eschborn, Germany.

GRA (2014), The Global Research Alliance website, *www.theglobalresearchalliance.org* (accessed 5 June 2014).

GRA (2012), "Global Research Alliance Inclusive Innovation" (brochure), GRA, *www.theglobal researchalliance.org/What-we-do/~/media/Files/Resources/What%20is%20Inclusive%20Innovation_Global %20Research%20Alliance.ashx*.

GRA (n.d.), *Global Research Alliance, overview* (brochure), GRA, *www.theglobalresearchalliance.org/en/~/ media/Files/GRA%20brochures/Global%20Research%20Allliance%20overview.ashx*.

Guaipatin, C. (2014), "A call for social innovation", presentation at the OECD-Growth Dialogue Symposium on Innovation and Inclusive Growth, 20 March 2014, Paris *www.oecd.org/sti/inno/Session_ 6_Guaipatin.pdf*.

Gupta, A.K. (2012), "Innovations for the poor by the poor", *International Journal of Technological Learning, Innovation and Development*, Vol. 5, No. 1/2.

Jaumotte, F. and N. Pain (2005), "Innovation in the Business Sector", *OECD Economics Department Working Papers*, No. 459, OECD, Paris.

Koh, H., A. Karamchandani and R. Katz (2012), *From Blueprint to Scale. The Case for Philanthropy in Impact Investing*, The Monitor Group, Cambridge, MA.

Krämer, A. and M. Herrndorf (2012), *Policy Measures to Support Inclusive and Green Business Models*, United Nations Global Compact and Donor Committee for Enterprise Development.

Krishna, V. (2014), "Inclusive Innovation and Development: Indian Experience", presentation at the OECD Innovation For Inclusive Growth Project Advisory Group Meeting on 19 March 2014, Paris, *www.oecd.org/sti/inno/Session%204_AdvisoryGroup_Krishna_India.pdf*.

Kubzansky, M., A. Cooper and V. Barbari (2011), *Promise and Progress. Market-Based Solutions to Poverty in Africa*, The Monitor Group, Cambridge, MA.

Mashelkar, R.A. (2014), "Accelerated Inclusive Growth through Inclusive Innovation", presentation at the OECD-Growth Dialogue Symposium on Innovation and Inclusive Growth, 20 March 2014, Paris, www.oecd.org/sti/inno/Session_3_Mashelkar_Keynote.pdf.

Massachusetts Institute of Technology (2014), MIT D-LAB website, http://d-lab.mit.edu/ (accessed on 23 April 2014).

Mendoza, R.U. (2011). "Why do the poor pay more? Exploring the poverty penalty concept", *Journal of International Development*, 23/1, pp. 1-28.

Mkhize, N. (2014), "Knowledge And Innovation For Inclusive Growth Project", presentation at the OECD Innovation For Inclusive Growth Project Advisory Group Meeting on 19 March 2014, Paris, www.oecd.org/sti/inno/Session%203_AdvisoryGroup_Mkhize_South_Africa.pdf.

National Innovation Foundation (2014), website, www.nif.org.in, accessed in March 2014.

OECD (2014a), "STI policy profiles: Innovation in firms", in *OECD Science, Technology and Industry Outlook 2014*, OECD Publishing, Paris, http://dx.doi.org/10.1787/sti_outlook-2014-en.

OECD (2014b), *OECD Economic Outlook*, Vol. 2014/1, OECD Publishing, Paris, http://dx.doi.org/10.1787/eco_outlook-v2014-1-en.

OECD (2014c), *National Intellectual Property Systems, Innovation and Economic Development: With perspectives on Colombia and Indonesia*, OECD Publishing, Paris, http://dx.doi.org/10.1787/9789264204485-en.

OECD (2014d), Purchasing power parities (PPP) (indicator), http://dx.doi.org/10.1787/1290ee5a-en, (accessed on 03 December 2014).

OECD/The World Bank (2014), *Making Innovation Policy Work: Learning from Experimentation*, OECD Publishing, Paris, http://dx.doi.org/10.1787/9789264185739-en.

OECD (2013a), *Commercialising Public Research: New Trends and Strategies*, OECD Publishing, Paris, http://dx.doi.org/10.1787/9789264193321-en.

OECD (2013b), "Competition policy and knowledge-based capital", in *Supporting Investment in Knowledge Capital, Growth and Innovation*, OECD Publishing, Paris, http://dx.doi.org/10.1787/9789264193307-7-en.

OECD (2013c), *The Internet Economy on the Rise, Progress since the Seoul Declaration*, OECD Publishing, Paris, http://dx.doi.org/10.1787/9789264201545-en.

OECD (2013d), "Synthesis of Responses Received to the Project Scoping Questionnaire" presented at the Knowledge and innovation Advisory Group Meeting, Istanbul, 24 October 2014, www.oecd.org/sti/inno/WebsiteText_SynthesisCountryResponses_1Nov2013.pdf.

OECD (2012a), "Innovation for Development: The Challenges Ahead", in *OECD Science, Technology and Industry Outlook 2012*, OECD Publishing, Paris, http://dx.doi.org/10.1787/sti_outlook-2012-7-en.

OECD (2012b), *Financing High-Growth Firms: The Role of Angel Investors*, OECD Publishing, Paris, http://dx.doi.org/10.1787/9789264118782-en.

OECD (2011a), "Together for Better Public Services: Partnering with Citizens and Civil Society", *OECD Public Governance Reviews*, OECD Publishing, Paris, http://dx.doi.org/10.1787/9789264118843-en.

OECD (2011b), *Opportunities, Challenges and Good Practices in International Research Co-operation between Developed and Developing Countries*, OECD Publishing, Paris.

OECD (2011c), *Demand-side Innovation Policies*, OECD Publishing, Paris, http://dx.doi.org/10.1787/9789264098886-en.

OECD (2010), "Unleashing Innovations", in *The OECD Innovation Strategy: Getting a Head Start on Tomorrow*, OECD Publishing, Paris, http://dx.doi.org/10.1787/9789264083479-6-en.

OECD (2009a), *Is Informal Normal? Towards More and Better Jobs in Developing Countries*, OECD Publishing, Paris, http://dx.doi.org/10.1787/9789264059245-en.

OECD (2009b), *OECD Patent Statistics Manual*, OECD Publishing, Paris, http://dx.doi.org/10.1787/9789264056442-en.

OECD/Department of Science and Technology (South Africa) (2007), *Integrating Science & Technology into Development Policies: An International Perspective*, OECD Publishing, Paris, http://dx.doi.org/10.1787/9789264032101-en.

OECD and World Bank (2009), *Innovation and Growth: Chasing a Moving Frontier*, OECD Publishing, Paris, http://dx.doi.org/10.1787/9789264073975-en.

Paunov, C. and D. Guellec (2015), "Innovation, Technological Change and Inclusive Growth", unpublished manuscript, OECD.

Paunov, C. and C. Lavison (2014), "How to Scale-Up Inclusive Innovation? Policy Lessons from a Cross-Country Perspective", *OECD STI Working Paper Series*, forthcoming.

Smith, A. (2014), "Scaling-up inclusive innovation: asking the right questions?", contribution to the OECD – Growth Dialogue Symposium on innovation and inclusive growth held on 20-21 March 2014, Paris, www.oecd.org/sti/inno/Session_3_Adrian%20Smith%20(paper).pdf.

Socialab (n.d.), Proyecta Colombia website, www.socialab.com/desafios/ideas/392# (accessed on 28 May 2014).

Society for Research and Initiatives for Sustainable Technologies and Institutions – SRISTI (2014), www.sristi.org (accessed on 28 May 2014).

UNGC and DCED (2012), *Partners in Development. How Donors Can Better Engage the Private Sector for Development in LDCs*, United Nations Global Compact, Bertelsmann Stiftung and United Nations Development Programme.

UNIID-SEA (2013), *Mapping and Evaluation of Innovation for Inclusive Development (IID) Initiatives in Indonesia*, Final Report, UNIID-SEA.

WIPO (2013), *Conceptual Study on Innovation, Intellectual Property and the Informal Economy*, Committee on Development and Intellectual Property, 11th Session, 13-17 May, Geneva

World Bank (2014a), Vietnam Inclusive Innovation project webpage (accessed on 3 June 2014), www.worldbank.org/projects/P121643/vietnam-inclusive-innovation-project?lang=en.

World Bank (2014b), "Promoting Pro-Poor Innovation in Vietnam", project webpage, last updated on February 2014, http://wbi.worldbank.org/sske/story/promoting-pro-poor-innovation-vietnam (accessed on 3 June 2014).

Chapter 4

The search for excellence and the democratisation of innovation

The chapter focuses on the role of innovation as a driver of growth and its contributions to inclusive growth. It discusses industrial and territorial inclusiveness, i.e. the proximity of innovation capacities across firms, sectors, regions, universities and public research institutes within countries. It goes on to describe how information and communication technology may support another trend – the "democratisation of innovation" – by increasing smaller firms' chances of succeeding with their innovations. It also discusses how new opportunities for "trickle-down" dynamics can improve industrial and territorial inclusiveness. It shows how policies may inadvertently lead to less industrial inclusiveness. It concludes by raising questions for future research.

Innovation is a critical driver of growth. As such, and as part of a wider set of structural policies, it will play a fundamental role in supporting inclusive growth. It can do so by driving income growth and job creation, which under certain conditions can benefit – directly or indirectly – all members of society, adding to the contribution of innovations specifically aimed at lower-income and excluded groups ("inclusive innovations"), discussed in Chapters 1-3.

Innovation-led growth – which is fundamentally a process of creative destruction – will have implications for industrial and territorial inclusiveness, i.e. the extent to which the distribution of innovation capacities evolves evenly across national firms, sectors, regions, universities and public research institutes. Agglomeration and reputation effects, as well as local externalities, reinforce this concentration. Forces supporting greater industrial inclusiveness are also at work: information and communication technologies (ICTs) have facilitated new opportunities for small-scale entrepreneurs to become successful innovators. Policy also shapes the concentration of innovation capacities within economies. Finally, industrial and territorial inclusiveness have impacts on inclusive growth, depending on how the entities concentrating innovation capacities connect with the rest of the economy, i.e. the extent of "trickle-down" mechanisms benefitting innovation.

Paunov and Guellec (2015) provides a more detailed discussion of innovation and its impacts on inclusive growth. Lembcke, Ahrend and Maguire (2015) discuss some of the spatial aspects of innovation and inclusive growth.

This chapter addresses several questions. What is inclusive growth, and how does innovation-driven growth contribute to inclusiveness? What is the evidence on "industrial inclusiveness" from the perspective of firms, sectors, universities or public research institutes, or regions? What are the trends in democratising innovation and driving more-effective trickle-down dynamics? How can policy foster industrial and territorial inclusiveness?

The remainder of the chapter is structured as follows: Section 1 discusses inclusive growth and how innovation supports such growth. Section 2 provides evidence on the factors supporting, or detracting from, industrial and territorial inclusiveness in developing, emerging and advanced economies. Section 3 elaborates on industrial opportunities and challenges for a reverse trend, the "democratisation of innovation". Section 4 evaluates opportunities for trickle-down dynamics. Section 5 discusses the impacts of innovation policies on inclusiveness. Section 6 presents questions that arise for future research. The final section concludes.

1. Inclusive growth and innovation

1.1. Definition

The OECD (2015) defines inclusive growth as "economic growth that creates opportunity for all segments of the population and distributes the dividends of increased prosperity, both in monetary and non-monetary terms, fairly across society". This report uses the term "social inclusiveness" to denote processes that create opportunities for all segments of the population, particularly people in the lower deciles of the income distribution and people who are otherwise excluded. Social inclusiveness is characterised by three dimensions: 1) multi-dimensionality; 2) an emphasis on distribution; and 3) policy relevance (Box 4.1).

> ### Box 4.1. **Characterising the OECD Initiative on Inclusive Growth**
>
> The following three dimensions characterise the approach adopted by the OECD Initiative on Inclusive Growth:
>
> - **Multidimensionality.** There is widespread recognition that gross domestic product (GDP) captures only part of economic welfare and excludes other dimensions that also matter for well-being, such as jobs, skills and education, health status, environment, civic participation and social connections (Stiglitz et al., 2009).
>
> - **Emphasis on distribution.** "Inclusive growth" means that people, independently of their socio-economic background, gender, place of residence or ethnic origin, should have fair opportunities to contribute to growth (i.e. they are part of the growth process), and that their contribution should yield equitable benefits (i.e. they benefit from the process outcomes). The specific emphasis on the "target" group to be "included" is very much a policy question specifically reflecting countries' socio-economic characteristics.
>
> - **Policy relevance.** Inclusive growth should be policy-actionable and make a link between policy instruments and the relevant monetary and non-monetary dimensions, taking into account distributional impacts. This requires in particular assessing the impact of policies and institutions on the different dimensions of inclusiveness, as well as the trade-offs and complementarities that are expected to exist between pro-growth and pro-inclusiveness policies.*
>
> * The OECD has done considerable empirical work to "map" – or establish causal linkages – between policies and outcomes, providing a rich body of evidence informing the work on inclusive growth. More information exploring the variety of channels can be found at: www.oecd.org/inclusive-growth.
>
> Source: OECD (2015), *All on Board: Making Inclusive Growth Happen*, OECD Publishing, Paris.

This report focuses on the role of innovation in shaping inclusive growth. Innovation refers to the "implementation of a new or significantly improved product (good or service), or process, a new marketing method, or a new organisational method in business practices, workplace organisation or external relations" (OECD/Eurostat, 2005). This definition does not in any way impose a "technology-based perspective" on innovation. Innovations may be incremental rather than radical, involving adjustments to existing products and technologies. This is critical to the report's discussion of opportunities for "democratising innovation" in this chapter and "inclusive innovation" initiatives in Chapters 1-3 of the report.

1.2. Growth, innovation and inclusive growth

Economic growth, poverty and inequality

Economic growth is critical to well-being, as it provides the resources that help create the conditions for more inclusive growth. As shown in Panel A of Figure 4.1, economic growth strongly correlates with a decline in poverty. According to World Bank data, 972 million people were living on less than USD 37.50 (United States dollars) per month in China in 1981; this number dropped to 157 million by 2009. India has also made substantial advances in reducing poverty: the official poverty ratio declined from 45% in 1994 to 37% in

Figure 4.1. GDP growth, poverty reduction and change in Gini coefficient
Per cent, percentage points and change in Gini coefficient[1]

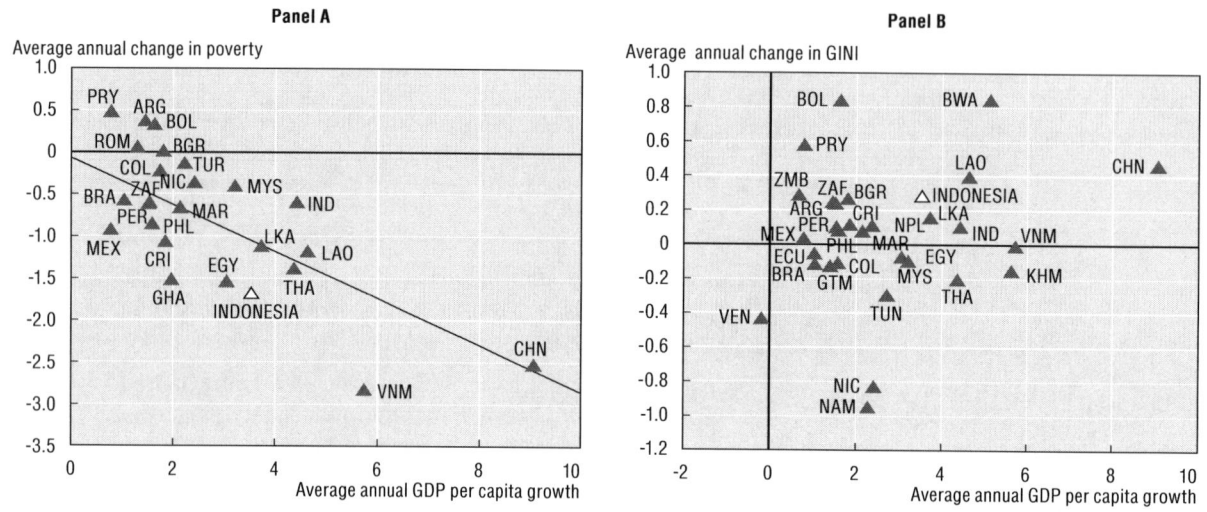

Note: GDP is GDP per capita at purchasing power parity (constant 2005 international dollars); poverty is the poverty headcount ratio at USD 2 per day (purchasing power parity, percentage of population); various periods, starting between 1981 and 1993 and ending between 2006 and 2011.

1. The Gini coefficient is a standard measure of inequality, where "0" means everybody has the same income and "1" means the richest person has all the income.

Source: World Bank (2014b), *World Development Indicators*, http://data.worldbank.org/data-catalog/world-development-indicators.

2005. Between 2005 and 2012 – a period during which India achieved the fastest rate of economic growth in its history and also implemented a number of policies aimed at helping the poor – extreme poverty declined to 22% of the population, or some 270 million people (Gupta et al., 2014).

Innovation plays a major role in ensuring sustained growth; productivity growth in particular contributes to employment and entrepreneurship opportunities. Neoclassical growth models identify knowledge accumulation and technological progress as the only way to achieve long-run growth and reduce the effects of diminishing returns to capital. Innovation can also directly support inclusive growth, by providing solutions to the challenges facing lower-income and excluded groups, as evidenced by multiple examples separate from inclusive innovations: during India's Green Revolution of the 1960s, innovation led to the introduction of high-yield plant varieties and seeds, and increased the use of fertilisers and irrigation. This resulted in a substantial increase in grain production, with the result of not only raising agricultural productivity, but also directly addressing food scarcity among the country's poor.[1] Nevertheless, eradicating poverty continues to be a major challenge for many emerging and developing economies: in 2010, an estimated 4.3 billion people in low and middle-income countries – i.e. 62% of the world's population – lived on less than USD 5 per day (World Bank, 2014a).

However, a country's growth performance does not necessarily in itself lead to greater inclusiveness, as shown by the mixed evidence on the relation between inequality (measured by the Gini coefficient, a frequently used measure of income concentration) and growth performance (see Panel B of Figure 4.1.). This is also clear from the disappointing performance of OECD countries, where income inequality has widened in recent years. In 2010, the income of the richest 10% was 9.5 times that of the poorest 10%; 30 years ago, it was only 7 times larger (OECD, 2011a, 2013a). The Gini coefficient also increased, from 0.29 in the mid-1980s to 0.32 in 2010 for the OECD.

The relative poverty rate after taxes and transfers, i.e. the ratio of people falling below the poverty line to the total population (applying a poverty line of 50% median income), increased in many OECD countries: 13 out of 17 countries for which data were available for both the mid-1980s and 2011 faced rising income poverty. Internal country trends have also been striking: in East Germany, relative poverty affected 20% of the population in 2009 – almost twice as many as in the West (OECD, 2014a). Further, the economic crisis has heightened market income inequalities in OECD countries.

The link between innovation and social inclusiveness is often more complex than can be gleaned from national data. Evidence from regional data on innovation shows a non-linear relationship between research and development (R&D) investment and regional inequality. TheOn average, the regions investing very heavily (more than 2% of their GDP) in R&D in 2004-06 had the highest levels of income inequality in 2010. Inequality was lower in regions with intermediate levels of R&D investment in 2004-06, but rose again at the bottom of the investment range (less than 0.8% of regional GDP spent on R&D) (Figure 4.2). This last category combines very diverse regions, including some small and medium-sized states in the United States often characterised by exports of natural resources or agriculture (e.g. Alaska or Louisiana), and economically lagging regions in southern Europe (e.g. southern Spain, southern Italy and Greece). Regional R&D intensity may also be a proxy for highly educated households and global firms, and not only R&D per se.

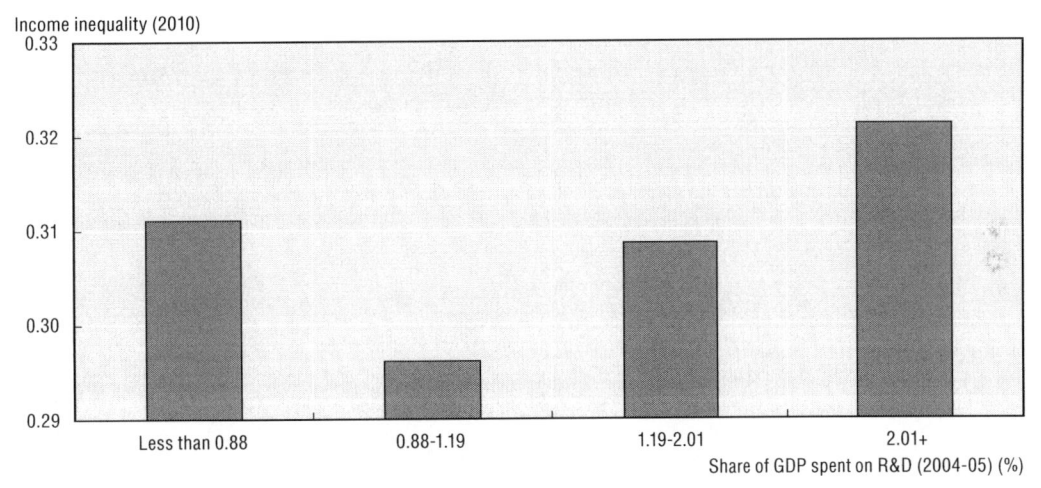

Figure 4.2. **R&D spending and income inequality after five years**

Source: Lembcke, Ahrend and Maguire (2015) using data from OECD (2013b), *Regional Statistics Database* (TL2). OECD large (TL2) regions represent the first administrative tier of subnational government (see OECD 2013d for further details). The bars depict average income inequality, measured by the Gini coefficient of disposable household income around 2010. Countries included are Australia, Austria, Belize, Canada, Czech Republic, Germany, Spain, Finland, France, Great Britain, Greece, Hungary, Italy, the Netherlands, Norway, Poland, Slovakia, Slovenia, Sweden and the United States. Data for disposable income refers to 2010 for all countries except Australia (2009-10), Finland (2011), Germany (2011), Norway (2011), Spain (2008-10 average), Sweden (2011) and the United States (2010-12 average). Groups are split by the average share of GDP invested in R&D investment over 2004-06.

2. Industrial inclusiveness

2.1. *Evidence on the concentration of innovation activities*

Industrial inclusiveness refers to the closeness of innovation capacities across firms, sectors, regions, universities and public research institutes within countries. Its opposite is the concentration of leading innovation capacities in firms, sectors, regions or universities of international standing that are highly advanced compared to others in the economy.[2] As described below, this concentration of innovation is important in developing, emerging and advanced economies alike.

Firms

The concentration of excellence among firms, especially within very narrowly defined sectors and regions, is characterised by the co-existence of very productive firms with weakly productive firms, productivity being closely related to innovation capacities. Microeconomic data point to substantial dispersion: in the United States, for instance, Syverson (2004) shows that "the plant at the 90th percentile of the productivity distribution makes almost twice as much output with the same measured inputs as the 10th percentile plant".[3] Hsieh and Klenow (2009) find the dispersion among firms in China and India to be even more substantial. Only a subset of firms operate with modern technologies, while a vast majority of firms are not productive enough to invest in technology upgrading and R&D (Hsieh and Klenow, 2009; Alfaro et al., 2009). The frontrunners are globally competitive and include the top R&D investors in the world, as well as some firms from emerging and developing countries (European Commission, 2013). As shown in Table 4.1, top performers from emerging economies include Huawei (China), Petrochina (China) and Tata Motors (India). Korea has 9 companies in the Top 500 of the EU Industrial R&D Scoreboard 2013, with the major *chaebols* (Korea's large business conglomerates) – Samsung (which invested USD 12 billion in R&D), LG (USD 2.6 billion) and Hyundai (USD 1.8 billion) – representing a substantial share of its total national R&D investments.

Table 4.1. **Top 15 firms from emerging economies in the EU Industrial Investment Scoreboard 2013**

No.	Firm	Sector of activity	Economy	R&D investment (in million USD)	Employment (in 1 000)
1	Huawei Technologies	Telecommunications equipment (9578)	China	2 392	110
2	PetroChina	Oil and gas producers (53)	China	1 774	553
3	China Railway Construction	Construction and materials (235)	China	1 407	229
4	Hon Hai Precision Industry	Electronic equipment (2737)	Chinese Taipei	1 314	n.a.
5	ZTE	Telecommunications equipment (9578)	China	1 188	85
6	Taiwan Semiconductor Manufacturing	Semiconductors (9576)	Chinese Taipei	1 006	33
7	Petroleo Brasiliero	Oil and gas producers (53)	Brazil	980	80
8	Vale	Mining (177)	Brazil	867	71
9	MediaTek	Semiconductors (9576)	Chinese Taipei	789	5
10	Gazprom	Oil and gas producers (53)	Russian Federation	781	393
11	China Petroleum & Chemicals	Oil and gas producers (53)	China	724	373
12	HTC	Telecommunications equipment (9578)	Chinese Taipei	438	13
13	Tata Motors	Automobiles and parts (335)	India	413	n.a.
14	CSR China	Commercial vehicles and trucks (2753)	China	366	80
15	Wistron	Computer hardware (9572)	Chinese Taipei	335	n.a.

Note: Ranking refers to the original ranking of 2 000 firms in the EU Industrial R&D Investment Scoreboard 2013. Exchange rate NC/EUR (national currency/euro): EU Industrial R&D Scoreboard 2013 (http://iri.jrc.ec.europa.eu/scoreboard13.html); exchange rate NC/USD: Bank of England (www.bankofengland.co.uk/boeapps/iadb/Rates.asp) for China, Chinese Taipei and India; exchange rate NC/USD: United States Federal Reserve (www.federalreserve.gov/releases/h10/hist/dat00_bz.htm) for Brazil.
Source: European Commission (2013), EU Industrial R&D Investment Scoreboard 2013, http://iri.jrc.ec.europa.eu/scoreboard13.html.

Another dimension of innovation concentration becomes apparent when observing the differences across firm size. In most countries represented in Figure 4.3, small to medium-sized enterprises (SMEs) account for less than 40 percent of total business

Figure 4.3. **BERD by size class of firms, 2011**
As a percentage of R&D performed in the business sector

[Figure: Bar chart showing percentages for countries — Firms with fewer than 50 employees and Firms with 50-249 employees. Countries listed: Estonia, New Zealand, Norway, Spain, Slovenia, Slovak Republic, Hungary, Canada, Czech Republic, Australia, Belgium, Poland, Portugal, Netherlands, Switzerland, Austria, Denmark, Korea, Italy, Chile, France, United Kingdom, Finland, Sweden, Luxembourg, United States, Germany, Japan.]

Source: OECD (2013c), OECD Science, Technology and Industry Scoreboard 2013: Innovation for Growth, OECD Publishing, http://dx.doi.org/10.1787/sti_scoreboard-2013-en.

expenditures on research and development (BERD). Estonia and New Zealand – where SMEs account for over two-thirds of total BERD – are the exceptions. Figure 4.4 shows similar evidence in relation to firms' ownership of trademarks and patents.

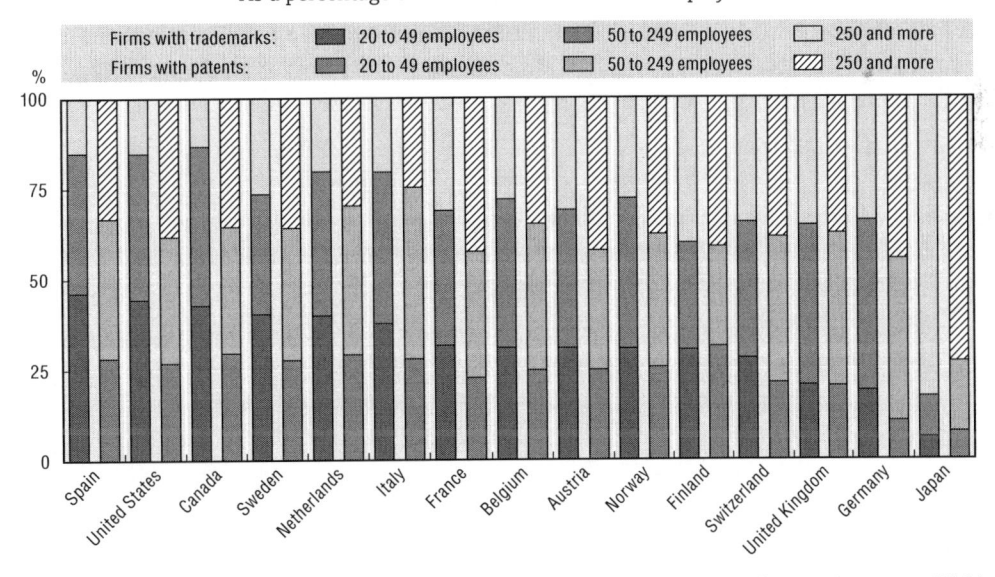

Figure 4.4. **Firms with trademarks and patents, by size, 2009-11**
As a percentage of firms with more than 20 employees

[Figure: Stacked bar chart. Firms with trademarks: 20 to 49 employees, 50 to 249 employees, 250 and more. Firms with patents: 20 to 49 employees, 50 to 249 employees, 250 and more. Countries: Spain, United States, Canada, Sweden, Netherlands, Italy, France, Belgium, Austria, Norway, Finland, Switzerland, United Kingdom, Germany, Japan.]

Source: OECD (2013c), OECD Science, Technology and Industry Scoreboard 2013: Innovation for Growth, OECD Publishing, http://dx.doi.org/10.1787/sti_scoreboard-2013-en.

Universities and public research institutes

A few leading universities and public research institutes also concentrate the contribution of public research to innovation. Their leadership often correlates with other high-performance indicators, notably teaching quality. Rankings such as the Academic Ranking of World Universities (known as the "Shanghai Ranking", introduced in 2003) and the Times Higher Education World University Ranking (launched in 2004) illustrate the heightened importance of competing for excellence among leading universities. Becoming a world-class research university generally requires long-term investments (Salmi, 2013).

Regions

In OECD countries, a limited number of regional innovation hubs concentrate innovation-related factors: over 33% of R&D takes place in the top 10% of large OECD regions[4] – which also concentrate around one-fourth of skilled employment[5] – and the top 10% of small OECD regions apply for 58% of patents (OECD, 2013d).[6] Concentration is even more pronounced in non-OECD countries: in China, the top three regions – Guangdong (46%), Beijing (14%) and Shanghai (13%) – account for almost three-quarters of all patenting activity. In India, the top three regions – Maharashtra (capital Mumbai) (26%), Delhi (24%) and Andhra Pradesh (13%) – account for almost two-thirds of national patenting activity (Creszenci et al., 2012).

Frontier research often takes place in centres of excellence, which by their very nature are tied to a place and (often) embedded in a local network. These centres create opportunities locally, but not evenly across the nation. Indeed, a closer look at the distribution of patenting activity – measured here by the number of patents filed under the Patent Cooperation Treaty (see OECD, 2009a, for details) – shows large regional differences. In China, for example, the majority of patents filed in regions along the coastline. In England or Germany, the southern regions are more active than the northern regions. In France and Spain, the regions around the capital cities of Paris and Madrid concentrate patenting activities (Figure 4.5).

The simple number of patents can create a skewed impression, however, since the more populated regions are more likely to produce a large number of patents. One indicator that is not affected by the size of a region is patent intensity, usually measured by the number of patents per million inhabitants. The difference between the number of patents and patenting intensity is most striking in China (Figure 4.5).

Other regional indicators, such as the share of regional scientific publications per 1 000 inhabitants, also show evidence of strong concentration. In 2010, the top 40 OECD regions (out of almost 1 700 Territorial Level 3 regions with data) represented one-third of all scientific publications (OECD, 2013b). A similar picture of concentration emerges for regional shares of R&D expenditure (Figure 4.6) (OECD, 2013d).

2.2. Factors determining the concentration of innovation

Innovation concentration is not a new phenomenon: it reflects the substantial economies of scale and scope resulting from agglomeration effects. However, the significant differences in the various dimensions of concentration require different approaches to addressing them. The co-existence of high-performing and low-performing firms in some markets is somewhat surprising, as competition could be expected to force bad performers out of the market. Weak competitive pressures, combined with lack of market integration, likely feature among the reasons why technology and productivity gaps across firms are greater in developing countries. In addition, framework conditions may particularly affect small firms and younger businesses, and thus generate a skewed distribution of innovative firms.

Other factors, this time related to the heterogeneous distribution of knowledge-based capital (KBC), contribute to the skewed distribution of innovations. Evidence from two

4. THE SEARCH FOR EXCELLENCE AND THE DEMOCRATISATION OF INNOVATION

Figure 4.5. **Regional distribution of innovative activity: Patents**

Number of patents filed under the Patent Cooperation Treaty in 2011

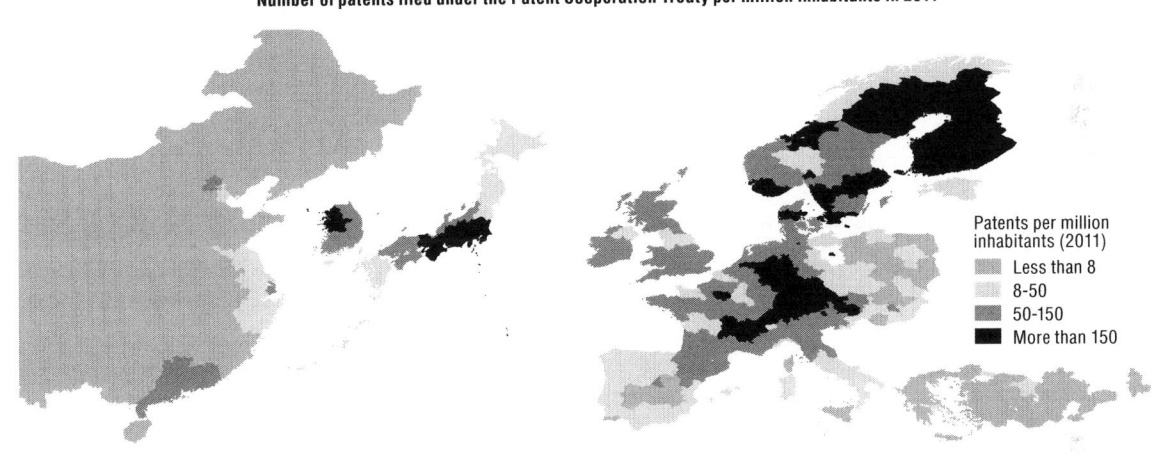

Patents (2011)
- Less than 15
- 15-80
- 80-300
- More than 300

Number of patents filed under the Patent Cooperation Treaty per million inhabitants in 2011

Patents per million inhabitants (2011)
- Less than 8
- 8-50
- 50-150
- More than 150

Source: OECD (2013b), *Regional Statistics Database* (TL2). Darker shades of blue indicate a larger number of patents (per million inhabitants). White regions indicate missing data. These maps are for illustrative purposes and are without prejudice to the status of sovereignty over any territory covered by these maps.

knowledge outputs – patents and/or publications – shows that only a very small share of ideas have high value, as measured by the number of citations they receive or other criteria (OECD, 2009a). A major factor why ideas translate into skewed value distribution relates to the non-rival and non-excludable nature of knowledge (Box 4.3) – marginal costs are low and therefore successful ideas easily capture entire markets, replacing all others. This occurs even more as markets become increasingly global.

These dynamics may in turn lead to a stronger concentration of innovation capacities among actors, since agglomeration and reputation benefits reward those generating winning ideas. Success often attracts not only talent, but also resources investing in the future generation of ideas. Chances are high that more leading innovations will emerge in areas where capacities are concentrated. This will reinforce certain actors' dominant role as generators of leading innovations, given that synergies arise from concentrating the best resources. These dynamics apply to both firms and universities. While they are particularly important in KBC-based industries – particularly the software industry – the important transformations of other sectors make them increasingly relevant to a broader group.

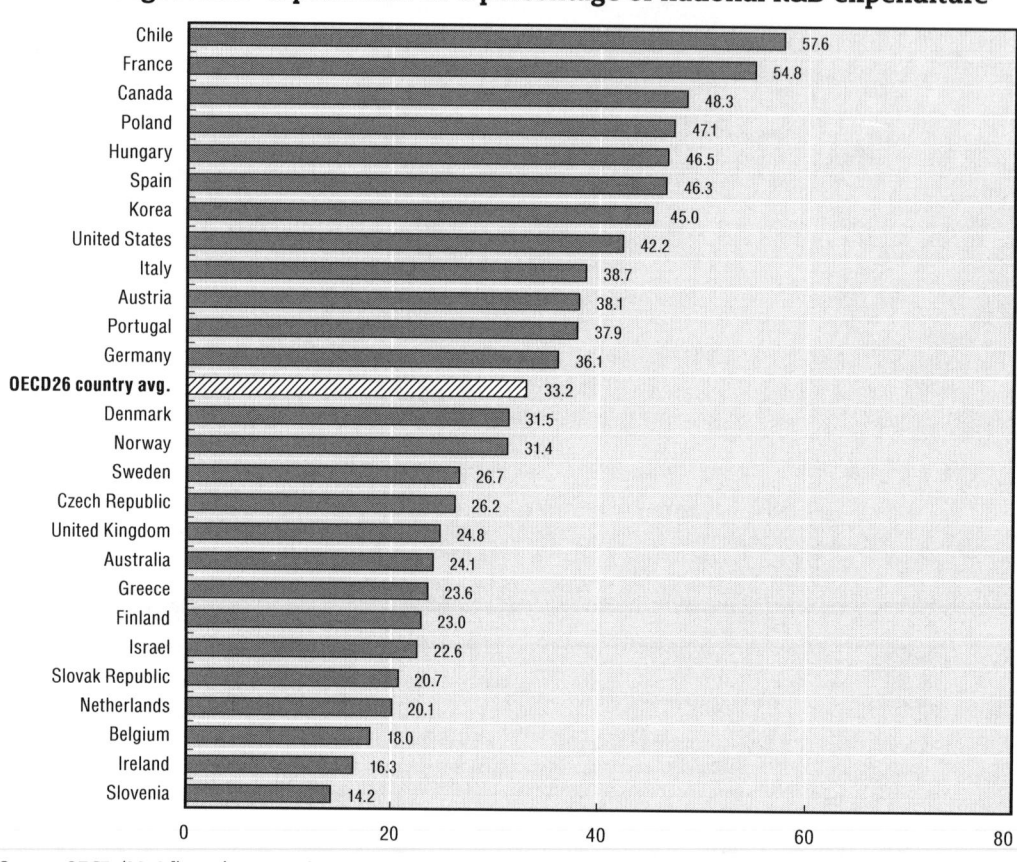

4. THE SEARCH FOR EXCELLENCE AND THE DEMOCRATISATION OF INNOVATION

Figure 4.6. **National R&D expenditure concentration by top 10% TL2 regions with largest R&D expenditure as a percentage of national R&D expenditure**

Country	%
Chile	57.6
France	54.8
Canada	48.3
Poland	47.1
Hungary	46.5
Spain	46.3
Korea	45.0
United States	42.2
Italy	38.7
Austria	38.1
Portugal	37.9
Germany	36.1
OECD26 country avg.	33.2
Denmark	31.5
Norway	31.4
Sweden	26.7
Czech Republic	26.2
United Kingdom	24.8
Australia	24.1
Greece	23.6
Finland	23.0
Israel	22.6
Slovak Republic	20.7
Netherlands	20.1
Belgium	18.0
Ireland	16.3
Slovenia	14.2

Source: OECD (2013d), *Regions at a Glance 2013.*, OECD Publishing, http://dx.doi.org/10.1787/reg_glance-2013-en.

Box 4.2. Caveats to interpreting statistics of industrial inclusiveness for policy purposes

From a purely technical point of view, the degree of dispersion depends on the size of the unit used as a measure of dispersion (for instance, different administrative levels of regions for regional inequalities, i.e. TL2, TL3 or TL4) and within which dispersion is analysed (e.g. whether firm dispersion is analysed within four-digit or two-digit industry categories).

Such differences are not negligible, as their meaning can vary greatly: high dispersion of very similar firms (e.g. firms producing similar products in the same location) points to potential shortcomings in competition policy, while dispersion among firms with different characteristics can point to various other explanatory factors (e.g. benefits from agglomeration, which render firms in dynamic clusters more productive than others). The levels of aggregation should, therefore, be considered before undertaking any assessment of a country's industrial inclusiveness. Moreover, some types of categorisations are sensitive to how boundaries are drawn at both the regional and industrial levels. For example, sector definitions vary substantially across industry classifications, and the recent classification revisions indicate how changes within industry can make alternative cut-offs relevant. This type of differentiation will critically shape some of the statistics.

> **Box 4.2. Caveats to interpreting statistics of industrial inclusiveness for policy purposes** *(cont.)*
>
> Moreover, a number of concentration statistics report statically and do not show the extent of movement from "outsiders" to "insiders" – a critical factor when exploring the implications of concentration on overall efficiency and the resulting dynamic opportunities. This is why it is important to integrate indicators of firm dynamics in the analysis. The extent to which dynamic factors shape concentration critically determines their impacts on growth and social inclusiveness-related objectives.

> **Box 4.3. The economics of knowledge**
>
> **Non-rivalry.** Knowledge is characterised as a non-rival factor of production, because the use of one piece of knowledge does not prevent the simultaneous use of the same piece by another party. Unlike physical goods, explicit knowledge can circulate and be kept at the same place simultaneously. This applies, of course, to disembodied knowledge, because of its intangible nature. Moreover, the marginal cost of implementing a piece of knowledge is close to zero, because once an invention exists there is no need to re-invent it, although there may be a need to adapt it to circumstances, e.g. with information circulating on the Internet. For this reason, knowledge can generate *spillovers*: once a piece of knowledge satisfies the standard economic return requested by investors, it can go on to produce additional value accruing to competitors or customers, who can derive further benefit. In terms of the *social optimum*, as many agents as possible should make use of existing knowledge. By contrast, the goal with respect to tangible property is to find the single best place for its use and identify which type of market or administrative mechanism will lead to its most efficient allocation. Given that knowledge can be used in several places at once, the goal is to determine all the places in which this unit of knowledge can be used efficiently, taking into account the direct or indirect costs. In view of this essential difference, the mechanisms allocating disembodied knowledge across the economy will differ deeply from those allocating tangible goods and factors.
>
> **Excludability and non-excludability.** When private parties produce explicit knowledge, they need to invest scarce resources in its production. Earning a return on the investment often depends on the ability of the private parties to exclude end users who will not pay for the knowledge. Thus, excludability is a key condition for earning private monetary value from explicit knowledge; this is where intellectual property (IP) can play a substantial role. The means used to assure excludability can be *technical*, such as protecting access through passwords; *legal*, under the form of copyright protection, patents and other types of IP; and *organisational*, including keeping the knowledge secret. The partially non-excludable characteristics of knowledge constitute a challenge for inventors, as spillovers do not allow them to recoup the costs of producing knowledge.
>
> **Enhancement over time.** Unlike physical property, knowledge grows over time. New knowledge expands based on the existing stock of knowledge, new discoveries rely on the current level of science, and new ideas originate from yesterday's experiences. Knowledge is non-rival and virtually impossible to destroy. Because knowledge can accumulate over time, it gives sense to the notion of knowledge capital. Unlike physical capital, knowledge capital is not depleted when used, although its monetary value may depend on usage.
>
> *Source:* OECD (2014b), *National Intellectual Property Systems, Innovation and Economic Development*, OECD Publishing, http://dx.doi.org/10.1787/9789264204485-en.

Agglomeration benefits have implications for territorial inclusiveness. Inventors' need to access specific infrastructure and production infrastructure also explain concentration. Imperfect financial market conditions outside of the leading agglomerations can hinder innovation efforts by other regions. These regions may not be able to match the same scale of innovation activities. Cities tend to produce the largest agglomeration benefits – the positive externalities arising from bringing many firms, workers and customers together in the same place. These benefits make firms and workers in large cities generally more productive than in small cities or rural areas. This means the same amount of inputs produces more output – which in turn results in higher GDP per capita – in larger cities (Box 4.4).

> ### Box 4.4. **Why is economic activity concentrated regionally?**
>
> Research into agglomeration benefits points to three core factors: 1) sharing; 2) matching; 3) learning.
>
> 1. Sharing of facilities or inputs by a large number of firms is one way of creating critical mass. The provision of certain goods or facilities requires a critical mass of beneficiaries. For example, branching a river to provide a constant stream of fresh water for an industrial site involves large fixed costs that are only worth paying if enough firms benefit from this investment. A similar argument applies to the provision of specialised goods and services. Specialisation requires demand that is large enough to sustain the business model.
>
> 2. Deeper labour markets, with a larger pool of potential workers, can result in a better match between job and worker. In other words, the person hired from a larger pool of applicants is likely to be more productive than the person from a smaller pool of applicants (Helsey and Strange, 1990). Location matters, as applicants mostly limit themselves to jobs around their current residence. For example, Marinescu and Rathelo (2014) show that more than 80% of users of the largest job search website in the United States submitted applications to firms in the same metropolitan area; 90% sent them to firms located less than 100 kilometres away from their place of residence.
>
> 3. Geographical proximity facilitates knowledge spillovers and learning. Formal – and especially informal – interactions benefit from people living and working close to one another. While innovation in ICTs generated large opportunities for wider knowledge spillovers (Paunov and Rollo, 2014), proximity continues to matter, particularly for effective collaboration. In 2013, global ICT leader Yahoo abolished its work-at-home policy in favour of creating greater interaction at the workplace (*New York Times*, 25 February 2014).
>
> The three mechanisms (sharing, matching and learning) lead to sizeable productivity benefits. Empirical estimates of the size of agglomeration benefits for 5 OECD member countries find that productivity in metropolitan areas the size of London or Chicago is on average about 20% higher than in small cities with 50 000 inhabitants (Ahrend et al., 2014). This estimate is representative of the range of estimates found in the academic literature (see Combes et al., 2011, for a review).
>
> *Source:* Ahrend, Lembcke and Maguire (2014).

The importance of spatial proximity for certain forms of innovation collaboration can also reinforce agglomeration forces. The propensity of inventors to co-patent with partners from the same region is higher than the propensity to co-patent with co-inventors from different regions within the same country or from abroad (Figure 4.7).

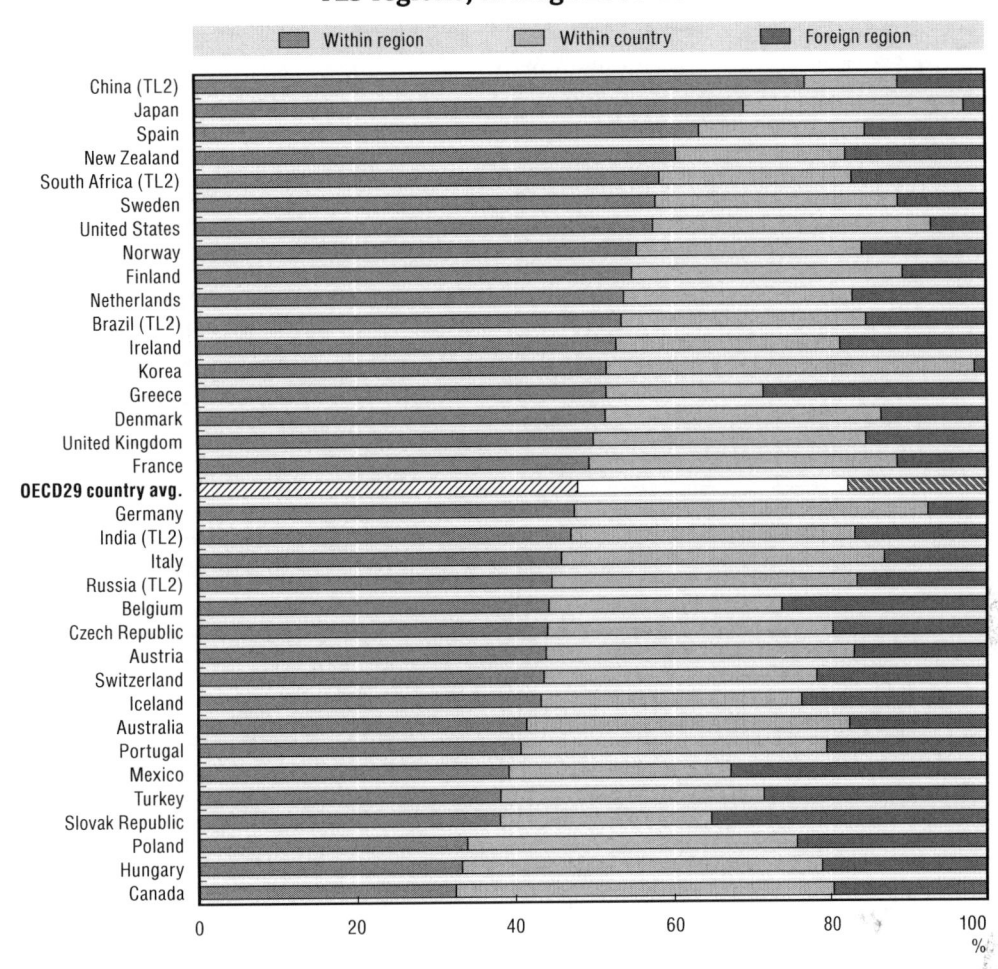

Figure 4.7. **Share of co-patents by location of partners, TL3 regions, average 2008-10**

[Bar chart showing share of co-patents (Within region, Within country, Foreign region) for the following countries/regions, from top to bottom: China (TL2), Japan, Spain, New Zealand, South Africa (TL2), Sweden, United States, Norway, Finland, Netherlands, Brazil (TL2), Ireland, Korea, Greece, Denmark, United Kingdom, France, OECD29 country avg., Germany, India (TL2), Italy, Russia (TL2), Belgium, Czech Republic, Austria, Switzerland, Iceland, Australia, Portugal, Mexico, Turkey, Slovak Republic, Poland, Hungary, Canada. X-axis from 0 to 100%.]

Source: OECD (2013d), *Regions at a Glance 2013*, OECD Publishing, http://dx.doi.org/10.1787/reg_glance-2013-en.

By contrast, the creative destruction that characterises innovation-based growth can challenge leaders' position in the global economy, lessening the concentration of innovative activities among owners of "winning ideas". Given the assets they can rely on, however, leaders may have an edge in maintaining their leadership – unless too many of their assets are stranded in existing facilities. At the same time, many governments have tended to concentrate their support on top actors to foster national competitiveness, further intensifying the concentration of innovation capacities.

3. The democratisation of innovation

The "democratisation of innovation" refers to the widening of the group of successful innovators to include actors who did not previously participate in innovation processes – particularly smaller entities, i.e. individuals, firms and entrepreneurs from a variety of backgrounds that are typically considered outsiders – and have opportunities to succeed with bottom-up initiatives. The extent to which these outsiders succeed in innovation is closely related to their ability to reach a sufficient scale – which is therefore at the heart of opportunities for more democratic innovation dynamics. Innovation policies can also create wide opportunities for the "democratisation of innovation". Turkey's National Science,

Technology and Innovation Strategy 2011-16 is an example of a policy framework that aims to do so by widening opportunities for SMEs to engage in innovation. Policy measures implemented to realise such potential include i) the Individual Entrepreneurship Multi-Phase Support Programme, a programme that provides grant-based financial support and mentorship, and ii) the SME R&D Grant Programme, which provides up to USD 250 0000 for SME's R&D projects.

While much innovation is highly concentrated, evidence also points to the reverse: Figure 4.8 shows that the share of young enterprises in innovation can be substantial, particularly when it comes to business-sector services in certain countries.

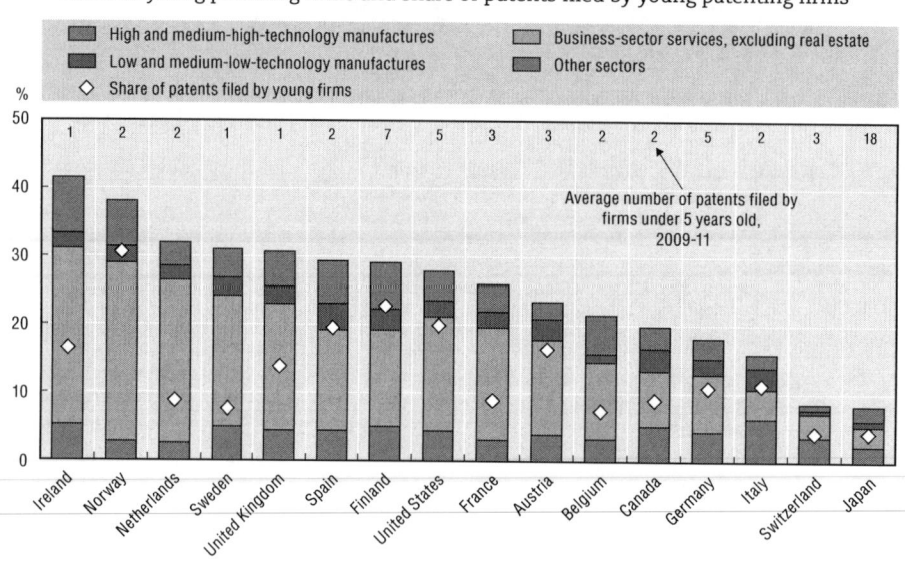

Figure 4.8. **Patenting activity of young firms by sector, 2009-11**
Share of young patenting firms and share of patents filed by young patenting firms

Source: OECD (2013c), OECD Science, Technology and Industry Scoreboard 2013: Innovation for Growth, OECD Publishing, http://dx.doi.org/10.1787/sti_scoreboard-2013-en.

3.1. ICT-based trends underlying the democratisation of innovation

Among the ICT-empowered trends that have helped democratise innovation, the following have played an important role:

- **Product distribution has become cheaper, reducing the cost of launching innovations.** This cost reduction simply stems from the fact that accessing customers on the Internet is less expensive than through brick-and-mortar stores. Dedicated digital distribution platforms, such as Apple's App Store for mobile apps, allow producers of mobile applications to sell their products directly to their main target audience. This effectively removes a substantial distribution and marketing cost for would-be entrepreneurs, particularly – though not solely – when selling non-material products. Similarly, Amazon offers third parties the opportunity to sell their products on its platform, while Facebook and Twitter (among others) facilitate targeted product marketing. This means that innovators can serve a larger customer base at much lower cost than previously, a development that provides smaller players with new distribution opportunities.

- **Innovation-related production costs have decreased in some sectors.** Software has helped reduce the costs of making high-quality products in a number of fields.

Musicians, for example, can now produce professional songs using software on a laptop, rather than paying to record them in a music studio. Software product development costs have also decreased: more baseline building blocks for creating new software products are available, and a number of platforms (e.g. oDesk) facilitate finding developers globally to create programming solutions. Cloud computing services – such as Amazon Web Services – provide high-quality data processing capacities without requiring large upfront investments, spurring a new dynamism of digital start-ups (The Economist, 2014). Moreover, 3D printing seems to hold the promise of lowering production costs, although some are sceptical of the actual overall potential of the method. Finally, the opportunity to outsource manufacturing production in global value chains (GVCs) may also provide savings opportunities. To date, most of these developments appear to have mainly benefited larger firms, but there are indications that smaller firms are also starting to derive advantages.

- **The risks and time span between product development and market launch have decreased for certain innovations**. Software start-ups, in particular, can open nearly instantaneously – and, if unsuccessful, wind their activities down rather easily. Market observers also point to opportunities for a more experimental approach to innovation, where innovators offer a multiplicity of products to consumers and adjust them based on information provided by test users. If convergence is achieved, they scale up the products fully, sometimes even globally. A number of online sites, such as UserTesting.com, also help companies experiment. Such approaches are particularly relevant when products are developed on platforms and rely on modularity, so that each new innovation is a less costly variation of an existing concept and may be available to the entrepreneur at little or no cost.

- **The demand for innovation can be assessed more easily**. An increasing amount of data is being collected about consumption behaviour, allowing firms to better understand demand for their products. Moreover, platforms such as InnoCentive (Box 4.5), which allow posting innovation challenges, can facilitate the innovation "crowdsourcing" of innovation. Segmenting product innovation also allows for wider participation, deepening technological markets. Finally, the opportunity to consult more systematically with users, and even the option of user-driven innovation, can arguably lower the costs associated with identifying demand.

- **Using the Internet facilitates access to knowledge for innovation**. Evidence shows these benefits arise particularly for businesses in developing countries, which were previously at a disadvantage in accessing formal or informal information. Platforms such as TechShop provide support for small-scale entrepreneurship, reducing the barriers to engaging in innovation.

More evidence will help inform how and where changes to the conduct of innovation will be strongest. Scale continues to matter in knowledge-based economies, but this time it relates to networks. The market value of large dominant players, e.g. Facebook, LinkedIn and Amazon, points to the critical role of companies that own platforms with large pools of followers.

Finally, in order for the Internet to play as critical a role in innovation activities across developed and developing economies alike, the development of backhaul and cross-border networks, which enable local networks to connect to the wider Internet, is critical. In several developing countries, communication networks often resemble rivers, with small branches of regional networks delivering their traffic to a central national backbone that ends at one submarine fibre, making cable cuts a greater risk to the functioning of the economy. Such

> **Box 4.5. InnoCentive: A new approach?**
>
> InnoCentive is an innovation platform that describes itself as the "world's largest marketplace for ideas". Its business model is based on the idea that firms, governmental agencies and non-governmental organisations (NGOs) can enhance their innovation process by tapping into global expertise. The company provides a platform where "seekers" can post an innovation challenge that is open to any "solvers", who can submit proposals and – if selected – receive the award associated with the project. So far, the platform numbers more than 300 000 solvers from nearly 200 different countries. More than 1 650 challenges have been posted and 40 000 solutions submitted. Over 1 500 prizes have been awarded, totalling over USD 40 million.
>
> Apart from providing the platform, InnoCentive's main role consists in facilitating IP transfer from solvers to seekers. InnoCentive also helps seekers formulate their challenges so as to attract relevant solvers and is involved in reviewing the submissions.
>
> A number of successes illustrate the potential advantages of the InnoCentive approach:
>
> - Prize4Life, an NGO that promotes the fight against amyotrophic lateral sclerosis – a neurodegenerative disease that has been neglected as a research by big pharmaceutical companies due to low profitability – issued a call for innovation. One of the respondents found a solution that led to the development of a disease biomarker.
> - Roche Diagnostics, a market leader in in-vitro diagnostics, decided to post challenges both internally – in its global R&D community – and externally – on InnoCentive. Candidate proposals submitted on InnoCentive were much more detailed, and on average of higher quality than the internal submissions. Moreover, a research problem that had persisted for 15 years was solved within 60 days of posting the challenge on the platform.
>
> Other platforms (e.g. NineSights and Idea Bounty) offer similar services, but are (to date) much smaller than InnoCentive.
>
> Source: InnoCentive (2014), InnoCentive website, www.innocentive.com, last accessed on 1 December 2014.

infrastructure shortcomings prevent Internet-based business development. The presence of data centres or other local facilities that can host Internet exchange points (IXPs) and servers is also essential (OECD, 2014e).

3.2. Other factors influencing the democratisation of innovation

The increased demand for more customised products – often including an important service component – may favour small, agile entrepreneurs with a smaller-scale innovation approach and the capacity to adjust to shifting demand. In other words, small firms might benefit from their ability to reduce information asymmetries between users and producers (Von Hippel, 2005). Adopting bottom-up and improvised approaches to innovation may also be more beneficial to competitive innovators than more inflexible innovation approaches centred on R&D departments' contributions to innovation (Radjou et al., 2013). Effectively small businesses do not have the constraint of a legacy business model, which may cause large businesses from changing their operations. There are numerous cases (as e.g. Kodak) such inertia ultimately threatened businesses' very survival.

Incremental and non-technological innovations for growth (compared to more technological innovations) offer wider opportunities for people who are not part of the professional elite to engage in innovation. At the same time, the growing number of highly skilled individuals has contributed to raising the pool of potentially successful small-scale innovators. This is relevant to the democratisation of innovation, which seeks to involve excluded groups in innovation processes.

Finally, higher levels of skills among groups of product "lead users" (possibly coupled with wider opportunities for developing products) allow consumers themselves to be more active as innovation producers (Von Hippel, 2005). This development can abolish some of the challenges posed by possible information asymmetries between producers and users, and sometimes even effectively stimulate entrepreneurship. The evidence on grassroots entrepreneurship described in Chapter 1 points to those opportunities.

Despite these developments, a number of trends point, on the contrary, to further concentration:

- The growing importance of GVCs might result in stronger concentration on a specific set of tasks – i.e. those in which a country's firms have a comparative advantage. Depending on the governance structures of GVCs, this can lead to an increasing concentration of innovation capacities among national actors. Large multinational corporations often dominate markets, and their smaller-scale suppliers depend on them as the sole buyers of their products. Concentration across actors in specific sectors appears all the more critical as countries seek to position themselves in GVCs and production specialisation becomes even more finely grained. These factors might reduce opportunities to democratise innovation more widely, since competing in international markets often entails substantial costs that small players cannot afford. At the same time, ICTs have eased conditions for smaller firms to participate in innovation processes (see, for example, Paunov and Rollo, 2014, and references therein).

- Industries whose success results from winning "innovation contests" may also lead to increased concentration. Larger firms might find it easier to engage in such contests, since they do not risk their very survival by engaging in innovation – particularly as they have diversified their investments in innovation, can rely on other sources of market income and do not rely on returns from their newly introduced innovations to survive (Fernandes and Paunov, forthcoming).

- Evidence shows that smaller firms, notably in developing economies, are much less efficient. This points to the potential benefits of concentrating efforts more deeply (Hsieh and Olken, 2014); in other words, efficiency in these economies would be better served by greater concentration than by the opposite. However, while the value of certain bottom-up activities has been widely debated – particularly with regard to grassroots innovation activities – many analyses conclude that this type of entrepreneurship critically improves the capacities of those involved, justifying support for grassroots innovation.

3.3. The relationship between concentration and the democratisation of innovation

Concentrating innovation activities and democratising innovation are not opposites. In many cases, innovation leaders are connected to – or even included in – broader innovation ecosystems comprising large and small, universities, etc., within such ecosystems. Democratisation can facilitate access to a wider community, which will share in the rewards of the wider ecosystem if it wins the race. Moreover, differences in scientific and/or technical domains influence both the opportunities for democratisation and the needs for concentration. The increasing costs of developing and deploying innovations in a number of fields – e.g. pharmaceuticals – may also lead to greater concentration in such sectors. By contrast, services innovations – particularly those in marketing or organisation – often require fewer investments.

4. Trickle-down dynamics: Diffusion and its impacts on industrial inclusiveness

4.1. Achieving diffusion

The distance between innovation leaders and the remainder of the economy depends on the ease with which leading-edge technologies are diffused across the economy. The extent to which such processes take place influences the gaps in innovation capabilities between insiders and outsiders. While wider diffusion fosters industrial inclusiveness – as well as social inclusiveness – a certain degree of exclusive reward to the innovator is needed to reward innovators. This is the very essence of the IP system, which provides inventors with exclusive rights to the rewards from their invention for a period of time. However, facilitating diffusion is essential to fostering the innovation process. Innovation and technical change depend on new knowledge because unlike physical property, knowledge grows over time. New knowledge expands based on the existing stock of knowledge ("standing on the shoulders of giants"), new discoveries rely on the current level of science, and new ideas originate from past experiences. Thus, to the extent that innovation ultimately depends on connecting to diverse sources of knowledge, its increased availability can provide wider opportunities for corporate innovation (Arthur, 2007).

The diffusion of innovation has several dimensions and tends to follow an S-shaped adoption curve: the innovation has lead users in the beginning and is more widely adopted in the medium term, after which the speed slows down as the market saturates and the innovation has been widely adopted. One interpretation of this delayed uptake relates to adopters' varying capacities: innovation leaders may be among the first to adopt the technology, which is subsequently adopted by firms further behind for which adoption requires greater effort. Similarly, on the demand side, many innovations initially only benefit the most affluent; later on, as their price decreases and the adoption mechanisms become better established, they also benefit poorer groups.

"Trickle-down" is not simply a matter of adopting existing products; it also often involves inclusive innovations that drive product adoption. Box 4.6 uses the historical example of medical innovations to illustrate the slow process of diffusing technologies and their impacts on well-being. The importance of innovations within the diffusion process is all the more critical when efforts are made to accelerate the benefit of new high technologies, such as 3D printing, for "bottom-up" innovation initiatives (see Chapter 1, Boxes 1.3 and 1.4).

Opportunities for leapfrogging suggest a differential approach to diffusion. They often arise in more excluded or laggard regions or groups in emerging economies that lack core infrastructure (including electricity or fixed-line telephone networks). New developments, such as mobile telephony, can allow leapfrogging, which might also benefit the laggards. Thus, adoption processes need not necessarily be linear and follow the same path as in other countries. In China, solar thermal heating – developed by Tsinghua University – has allowed bypassing gas or electricity-based heating in a number of rural areas and provided novel opportunities for competitiveness (Lee, 2014).

Several factors determine spillovers. The most crucial is the relevance of a given "island of excellence" and its specific innovation expertise to the remainder of the economy. Actors operating in the same activity will likely stand to benefit from new production technologies and other innovations, as will those relying on inputs from an "island of excellence". Companies supplying innovation leaders may equally stand to benefit, as the leaders may drive their suppliers to adopt certain production quality standards. The challenges in obtaining such gains have been debated extensively in the context of natural

Box 4.6. Medical innovations and social inequalities: The diffusion of health technologies in the 17th and 18th centuries

Between the 1600s and the early 1800s, the British elite's life expectancy at birth increased by 25 years (Figure 4.9) – more than 100 years before the overall population was able to extend its lifespan by the same amount.* Prior to the 1600s, the life expectancy of elites was no higher than that of the population at large – in fact, it was even lower for the royal families, owing in particular to the higher health risks (such as exposure to epidemics) of living in urban areas.

The gains over time stemmed from progress in medical research. Unlike in Continental Europe, the British elites started funding physicians and surgeons to conduct research, which ultimately led to increased life expectancy. English medical practitioners' integration in European information networks also allowed them to benefit from progress made outside the kingdom.

Figure 4.9. Average life expectancy at birth for British elites compared with the general population, 1500-1919

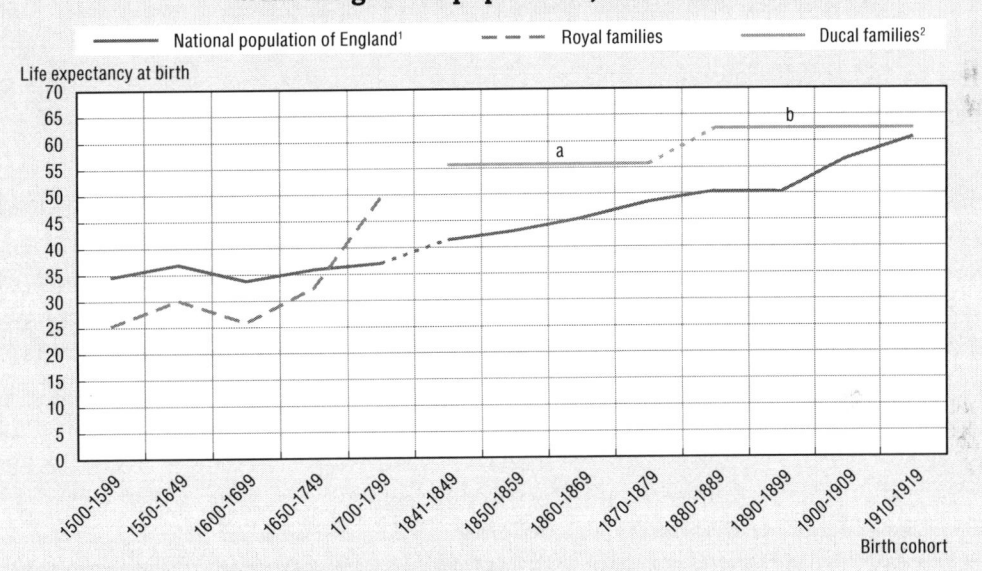

1. England only before 1799, England and Wales for 1841 on.
2. Ducal families life expectancies correspond to averaged males and females life expectancies for birth cohorts 1830-1899 (a) and 1880-1934 (b).

Source: David et al. (2010) for the royal families and national population of England, birth cohorts until 1799; Human Mortality Database (2014, www.mortality.org), for the national population of England and Wales, birth cohorts after 1841; Hollingsworth (1957) for the ducal families; the data used correspond to non-weighted averages of male and female expectations of life at birth, as calculated by the author.

By 1700, the range of disease-specific innovations produced enabled innovative physicians to prevent, manage or cure many acute infectious diseases (e.g. plague, malaria, scurvy, smallpox or bloody diarrhea) that were common causes of death (Johansson, 2010). Much was gained from seeing fever as a symptom rather than an illness and curing it by keeping patients in cooler – rather than overheated – rooms.

Diffusion of such progress to the wider population did not occur rapidly, since a number of the most efficient cures were imported from South America and other remote locations

> **Box 4.6. Medical innovations and social inequalities: The diffusion of health technologies in the 17th and 18th centuries** (cont.)
>
> and were therefore very costly. Nevertheless, some constraining factors could have been avoided. For example, physicians used their control over certain practices and prices to extract rents (e.g. inoculations for smallpox were kept at a higher price by including them in complex treatment processes). Certain social practices and prejudices also hindered quick adoption: while changing the general population's hygiene habits also reduced the risks of contracting deadly diseases, lack of education partly delayed uptake.
>
> * Adult mortality declined first, beginning with men; the mortality of adult women only started to decline nearly a full century later. The life expectancy gap between men and women at age 25 is 14.9 years for the birth cohort of 1600-99, dropping to 2.1 years for the next cohort. Infant and child mortality dropped significantly during the 18th century. This is not only related to specific health challenges – particularly maternal health and childbirth – but also to research that initially focused on diseases affecting mainly men. Concerns over modesty delayed research on feminine health issues and prevented even the wealthiest women from accessing the best medical treatment. As women's health became a medical specialty in the 19th century (Johansson, 2010), the mortality rate of royal adult women caught up with the mortality rate of men.
>
> Source: Johansson (2010); Harris (2004).

resource industries – which are often disconnected from other national industries and may therefore have few spillover effects on the economy

4.2. New opportunities for knowledge spillovers

Knowledge spillovers are a critical contributor to diffusing innovation from insiders to outsiders, thereby enhancing overall performance. Wider opportunities for knowledge spillovers have been shown to have positive impacts on firms' performance (for overviews of the literature on international and geographic dimensions of knowledge spillovers, see Audretsch and Feldman, 2004; Keller, 2004). Bloom et al. (2013) find evidence in the United States of positive technology spillovers from R&D investments and show that the social returns from R&D are at least twice as high as the private returns. Knowledge lends itself to such spillovers: once created, it can be replicated and disseminated at virtually no cost, and benefits more firms than its original creator (Arrow, 1962).

Geographic proximity can play an important role in knowledge spillovers (Krugman, 1991; Audretsch and Feldman, 1996). Even for knowledge that is codified in the form of patents, there is a rich literature documenting that patent citations are geographically localised, a fact that holds true when controlling for the pre-existing concentration of technologically related activities (Jaffe et al., 1993). In some countries, the success of regional hubs in matters of innovation results in innovation-related or economic benefits in nearby regions. However, this is not always the case and depends in part on regional absorption capacity and agglomeration dynamics as illustrated by the cases of India and China (Box 4.7). Evidence in OECD countries notes that inter-regional spillovers from R&D investment depend in part on the characteristics of the neighbouring region, notably rural region neighbours appear to benefit more economically than neighbouring urban regions, the latter being more likely to compete for key resources (Lembcke, Ahrend and Maguire, 2015).

The increased opportunities provided by the widespread uptake of ICTs can reduce the barriers to transmitting increasingly sophisticated pieces of knowledge (Box 4.8).

> **Box 4.7. Inter-regional innovation benefits: The examples of China and India**
>
> Both China and India have experienced significant transformations in national innovation performance in recent years. They have rapidly increased their patenting activity, although it is highly unequal across regions and increasingly concentrated in a few leading regions. Nevertheless, their models of regional innovation systems illustrate different drivers and capacities for inter-regional spillovers.* These may partly relate to different sectors of activities, with China being more engaged in manufacturing and India more successful in services.
>
> - **In China,** the concentration of innovation reflects a traditional agglomeration story. Not only do richer regions with an intense agglomeration of activities, good infrastructure and a greater degree of industrial specialisation have higher patenting rates, they also absorb innovative capabilities from neighbouring areas. When taking into account agglomeration effects, however, the R&D spillovers from these regions become negative and significant. Thus, the agglomeration of innovation in core areas leads to greater concentration of innovation by promoting the outflow of knowledge from neighbouring regions.
>
> - **In India,** by contrast, R&D investment generates knowledge spillovers that cross state boundaries. The territorial configuration of innovation is more dispersed than in China, both quantitatively and qualitatively; the pattern of innovation across states is shaped by a combination of regional R&D investment and social conditions. The geography of innovation may nevertheless evolve in the future towards an even greater divide between innovative and globalised regions and the rest, possibly with the emergence of some "mid-sized" innovative centres alongside the mega-urban areas (such as Delhi and Mumbai).
>
> * Spillovers here are measured by patenting intensity (patents per capita), which has certain limitations in assessing innovation in a broad sense.
>
> Source: Based on Crescenzi, R., A. Rodríguez-Pose and M. Storper (2012), "The territorial dynamics of innovation in China and India", *Journal of Economic Geography*, Vol. 12, pp. 1055-1085.

> **Box 4.8. Evidence on the impact of the uptake of the Internet on firms in developing countries**
>
> In addition to households, many firms in developing and emerging countries have adopted the Internet to support their operations. Evidence from a recent dataset – described in further detail in Section 3 of Rollo and Paunov (2014) – shows that over 2006-11, a large share of firms used the Internet to communicate with clients and suppliers. Even in low-income economies, 47.3% of firms had adopted this communication tool. Moreover, while small and young firms used the Internet less actively than their larger counterparts, the uptake stood at 44.5% even among the smallest firms (Figure 4.10). Informal businesses were also active users of mobile telephony. Table 4.2 shows that the sampled African businesses in particular showed uptake despite substantial challenges: more than two-thirds had experienced power outages, and more than one in four firms did not use electricity. This indicates that more than previous technologies, ICTs provide opportunities for connecting and integrating a much larger group of innovators.

4. THE SEARCH FOR EXCELLENCE AND THE DEMOCRATISATION OF INNOVATION

> **Box 4.8. Evidence on the impact of the uptake of the Internet on firms in developing countries** (cont.)
>
> Figure 4.10. **Share of firms communicating with clients and suppliers through e-mail in 2006-11**
>
> In percentages
>
> | Category | Percentage |
> |---|---|
> | High income economies | 93.3 |
> | Upper-middle-income economies | 83.8 |
> | Lower-middle-income economies | 57.0 |
> | Low income economies | 47.3 |
> | Africa | 45.1 |
> | Eastern Europe and Central Asia | 77.7 |
> | Latin America and the Caribbean | 86.7 |
> | East Asia Pacific | 61.1 |
> | South Asia | 43.3 |
> | Micro (1-10 employees) | 44.5 |
> | Small (11-50 employees) | 72.6 |
> | Medium (51-150 employees) | 90.8 |
> | Large (more than 150 employees) | 96.9 |
> | Manufacturing | 70.3 |
> | Services | 66.6 |
> | Located in capitals | 75.3 |
> | Cities with > 1 million inhabitants | 70.2 |
> | Cities with > 250 000 and < 1 million inhabitants | 65.1 |
> | Cities with > 50 000 and < 250 000 inhabitants | 63.5 |
> | Cities with < 50 000 inhabitants | 72.8 |
>
> *Note:* Statistics provided are obtained for 50 013 firms from 117 developing and emerging economies as described in Paunov and Rollo (2014).
>
> Table 4.2. **Statistics on technology use of the informal sector**
>
> | | Overall | | AFR | | LAC | |
> |---|---|---|---|---|---|---|
> | | Firm Nbr. | Per cent | Firm Nbr. | Per cent | Firm Nbr. | Per cent |
> | *Use of cell-phone* | | | | | | |
> | No | 1 026 | 40.7 | 295 | 23.8 | 674 | 58.0 |
> | Yes | 1 495 | 59.3 | 943 | 76.2 | 489 | 42.1 |
> | *Use of electricity* | | | | | | |
> | No | 553 | 24.9 | 369 | 29.7 | 178 | 20.7 |
> | Yes | 1 668 | 75.1 | 873 | 70.3 | 681 | 79.3 |
> | *Experienced power outages* | | | | | | |
> | No | 765 | 46.1 | 275 | 31.8 | 489 | 72.0 |
> | Yes | 894 | 53.9 | 591 | 68.2 | 190 | 28.0 |
>
> *Note:* Information is based on firm observations for 14 countries: Angola, Argentina, Botswana, Burkina Faso, Cameroon, Cape Verde, Democratic Republic of Congo, Ivory Coast, Guatemala, Madagascar, Mali, Mauritius, Nepal and Peru.
> *Source:* World Bank Enterprise Surveys for 2006-11, Detail is provided in Paunov, C. and V. Rollo (2014), "Has the Internet Fostered Inclusive Innovation in the Developing World?", unpublished manuscript.

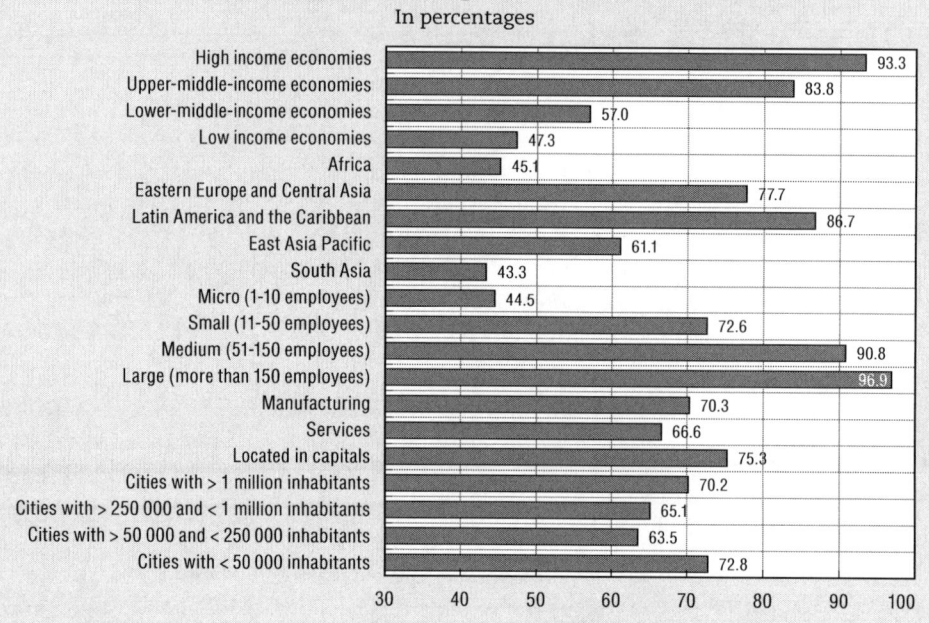

Videoconferencing is one means of transferring ever-larger amounts of information in ways that match the concept of "proximity". Firms with weaker access to "offline" knowledge networks (e.g. firms in remote locations) may have more to gain from Internet-enabled knowledge spillovers. This points to the possible benefits of the Internet in helping to democratise innovation by enhancing lagging performers' opportunities to compete with top performers. The evidence also confirms earlier studies showing that smaller firms, rather than larger ones, benefit more from spillover effects (see for example Acs et al., 1994).[7] The Internet also facilitates spillover benefits for researchers and their universities. Ding et al. (2010) show that the Internet facilitated the inclusion of women scientists, as well as the overall research output of people working at non-elite institutions, by providing increased access to the knowledge of others and larger opportunities for collaboration. Agrawal and Goldfarb (2008) also find that the adoption of Bitnet, an early version of the Internet, disproportionately benefitted middle-tier universities by increasing their collaboration with leading universities.

Several case studies illustrate how informal and grassroots innovators derived advantages from the Internet and mobile networks. In their study on Uganda, Muto and Yamano (2009) show that farmers located farther away from the country's centre gain more from these networks – independently of whether they themselves own mobile phones – effectively finding evidence of spillover effects from such infrastructure. Studies have also shown that micro-enterprises – including those operating in the informal sector – tend to benefit from ICTs, notably through mobile phones (see for example Duncombe and Heeks, 2002, on Botswana; Donner, 2004 and 2006, on Rwanda; Esselaar et al., 2004, for a survey of 13 African countries). Just as mobile technology and ICTs have served development, so can exploiting big data (OECD, 2009b, 2010, 2013e). The OECD initiative on Big Data for promoting growth and well-being will provide further insights into these questions (OECD, 2014d).

Such opportunities have caveats, in that knowledge networks alone often do not guarantee corporate performance – which is instead also driven by firms' own "absorptive capacities". The limitation of knowledge flows in the context of low internal capacities has been a core theme in the literature on knowledge spillovers (e.g. Görg and Greenaway, 2004). Firms need the capacity to deal with the knowledge they access, otherwise they have little to gain (Hu et al., 2005; Kokko et al., 1996). This is because knowledge often has a "tacit" component that cannot be easily transferred, or might be inappropriate in specific firm contexts requiring adjustments. Moreover, framework conditions might affect businesses differentially. The heterogeneous impacts of framework policies on firms have been a core theme of the OECD DynEmp Project.[8] One of its findings has been that conditions have often been difficult for young innovative firms, which have consequently been relatively more affected by the global crisis. Regarding the potential heterogeneous effects for laggards, Agrawal and Goldfarb (2008) find that the Internet is also an effective complement (rather than a substitute) to the advantages provided by larger agglomerations.

Econometric evidence provided by Paunov and Rollo (2014) shows that industry's adoption of the Internet has positive impacts on firms' labour productivity and investments in equipment, as well as minor benefits for innovation performance. Interestingly, the evidence points to larger gains for non-exporters, single-plant firms and those located in smaller agglomerations. The fact that the Internet benefitted more firms that commonly engage less in innovation points to the Internet's potential in facilitating the democratisation of innovation. However, quantile regression analysis – a statistical analysis that allows testing whether productivity differences affect impact differentially – shows that the more productive firms gained more than others, and that gains were low for all firms with lower productivity levels. Thus, while the evidence illustrates the opportunities provided by the Internet, these need to be combined with efforts to support firms' absorptive capacities; otherwise, they will have little to gain from the wider access to knowledge provided by the Internet.

5. The impacts of innovation policies on inclusiveness

Innovation policies have different outcomes on industrial and territorial inclusiveness depending on how they interact with other policy measures and framework conditions.

5.1. Exclusion effects of policies owing to implementation

Several design/procedural aspects can ultimately shape the impacts of innovation policies on exclusion. Irrespective of objectives, policies can have different outcomes and may contribute to excluding certain individuals/groups by virtue of their design, which may feature: 1) lengthy or costly application procedures before rewards are provided (hindering start-ups); 2) complex application procedures requiring expertise possessed only by selected firms; 3) rewards for past performance in subsequent application procedures (advantaging incumbents); 4) insufficient focus on advertising the existence of policy programmes to outsiders (potentially reducing the share of external participants); and 5) budgetary cuts affecting the amounts of available funding, potentially resulting in greater applicant selectivity. The same issue applies to territorial inclusiveness, as innovation policies that target specific sectors, social challenges or types of institutions will have a *de facto* place-based dimension that can add to, or detract from, inclusiveness. Certain programme rules, such as matching regional funds requirements, can also reinforce the flow of public innovation funding to the leading regions. While policy discussions often disregard these policy aspects, they are critical to how the policies will serve industrial or territorial inclusiveness, since they tend to aggravate "exclusiveness".

This challenge affects advanced, emerging and developing economies alike. It is often much easier and more straightforward to identify the largest contributors to innovative potential than the smallest. Moreover, past performance (e.g. using publication track records feature to select research excellence initiatives) is a simple selection criterion, as predicting potential future success is more challenging and involves greater risk. The challenges can be greater in developing and emerging economies, since selection criteria often exclude informal-sector participants.

5.2. Interaction effects with other policy measures and/or framework conditions

Biases in supposedly neutral innovation policies in the absence of complementary policies

Complementary policies supporting the policy environment in which firms operate can be critical to creating conditions for democratising innovation. The example of policies pertaining to IP rights illustrates this well. Even though IP rights provide opportunities for different actors, large businesses often use them more intensively. One reason is that enforcement costs are a significant hurdle for small companies, since the costs are not proportional to firm size; attorney fees, management costs and the time required to deal with litigation issues can be substantial. The size of firms' patent portfolios can help avoid costly litigation by using cross-licensing strategies,[9] meaning that small firms are at a disadvantage compared with larger firms – which can also reach agreements more easily thanks to repeated interaction with their competitors (Lanjouw and Schankerman, 2004). To make things worse, the fact that smaller companies are less prepared to withstand litigation increases their risks of facing further litigation. Meanwhile, the lack of capacities to manage and negotiate IP portfolios imposes a sunk cost that hinders smaller firms' ownership of IP rights. Corrupt business environments have also been shown to affect smaller firms' ownership of IP titles (Paunov, 2014). Moreover, IP rights are only useful to businesses if they can use IP-protected inventions to generate innovations; this requires financial resources small firms might not possess. Thus, IP may only serve the largest firms, unless complementary policies are in place. The importance of the interaction effects highlights the critical role of implementing a whole-of-government approach. This is insufficient in a scenario where policy interactions, matter regarding who will benefit from their implementation.

Another example of a policy instrument that may have biases is R&D tax credits: Governments can choose among various instruments to promote business R&D. In addition to giving grants or loans and procuring R&D services, many also provide fiscal incentives. Tax incentives for business R&D expenditures include allowances and credits, as well as other forms of advantageous tax treatment such as allowing for the accelerated depreciation of R&D capital expenditures. Today, 27 of the 34 OECD countries and a number of non-OECD economies give preferential tax treatment to R&D expenditures and do so in many different ways. Multinational enterprises (MNEs) benefit the most, as they can use tax planning strategies to maximise their support for innovation. This can create an unlevel playing field that disadvantages purely domestic and young firms. In response, Australia, Canada, France, Korea, the Netherlands and Portugal give more generous treatment to SMEs than to large firms. Well-designed direct subsidies may also support small businesses.

Impacts of business conditions

Policies also have differential impacts depending on the company's local environment, and particularly on whether firms have access to critical ingredients for innovation (including finance, human capital, knowledge and infrastructure). Access to these critical ingredients can vary within a metropolitan area or region within the same country. Access to sources of both finance and knowledge is a key requirement for innovators. Larger innovators have the opportunity to internalise some of these sources (e.g. by creating their own R&D labs and relying on internal resources to support innovation investments). By contrast, smaller firms rely on external sources, as they do not have sufficient own resources to internalise them. Especially in developing and emerging countries, business framework conditions can constitute stumbling blocks for companies' innovation performance, particularly that of smaller and catching-up firms (Tybout, 2000).

Evidence from India shows that liberalisation mainly benefitted large businesses, as framework conditions were still cumbersome. India's liberalisation reforms of the early 1990s were a catalyst for corporate R&D investments. By 1995, private investment in R&D across manufacturing firms was 14 times greater than in 1990. The growth of R&D investments was driven by a substantial rise in the number of innovating firms, from 3% in the late 1980s to 27% in 1999 (Figure 4.11). However, the share of firms investing in R&D increased much more substantially among larger firms. An econometric analysis shows that industrial

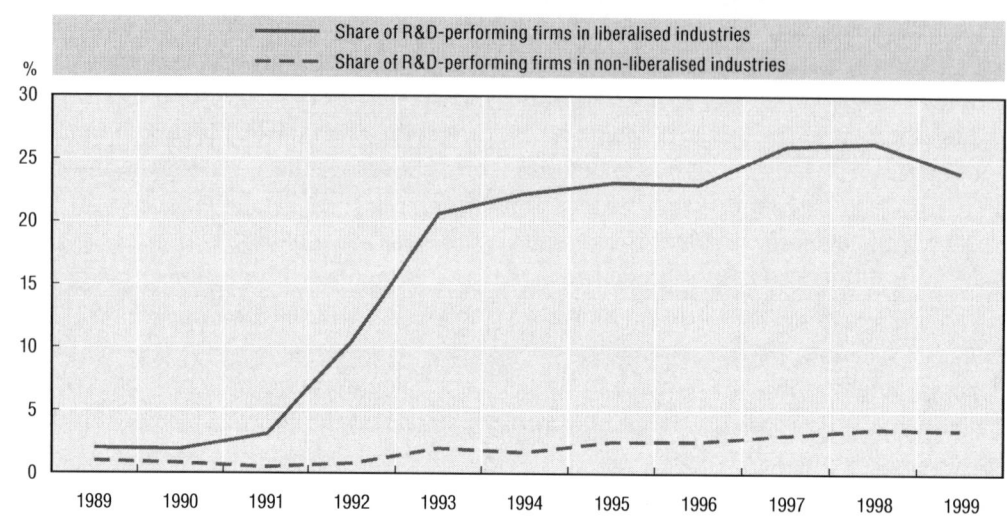

Figure 4.11. Share of R&D-performing firms in liberalised versus non-liberalised industries in India

[Line chart showing share of R&D-performing firms in liberalised industries rising from ~2% in 1989 to ~25% by 1997-1999, while non-liberalised industries remain near 0-3% throughout 1989-1999.]

Source: Bas and Paunov (2014), based on the *Prowess Database*.*
* Prowess (https://prowess.cmie.com) is the largest database of financial performance of Indian Companies.

liberalisation increased by 14% the probability of greater R&D investment by larger firms, but decreased by 8% the probability of R&D investment by smaller firms.

Results from the econometric analysis suggest barriers to firm operations drive the unequal effects of liberalisation: Table 4.3 shows that the largest group of firms benefit exceptionally only in environments with less developed economies and a weak knowledge and skills base. The findings highlight the importance of complementary policies in supporting smaller businesses' innovation efforts.

Table 4.3. Economic conditions and their impacts on innovation
Regression results indicating impacts of India's liberalisation reform on firms' R&D investments

	Economic development		Financial development		Knowledge base	
	High (1)	Low (2)	High (3)	Low (4)	High (5)	Low (6)
Liberalisation* Small firms	-0.123 (0.088)	-0.056 (0.051)	-0.084 (0.064)	-0.043 (0.076)	-0.091 (0.113)	-0.067 (0.048)
Liberalisation* Medium-small firms	-0.110 (0.093)	-0.053 (0.040)	-0.093 (0.068)	-0.012 (0.072)	-0.076 (0.127)	-0.059 (0.036)
Liberalisation* Medium-large firms	-0.033 (0.094)	0.056 (0.044)	0.009 (0.076)	0.063 (0.068)	0.014 (0.123)	0.040 (0.040)
Liberalisation* Large firms	0.052 (0.091)	0.185*** (0.059)	0.119 (0.074)	0.183** (0.074)	0.073 (0.121)	0.177*** (0.050)
Observations	7,597	8,610	8,277	7,930	4,792	11,415
R-squared	0.27	0.33	0.33	0.27	0.32	0.29

Note: The estimations include firm level controls, as well as firm and industry-year fixed effects. They are obtained using data from the *Prowess Database*. Standards errors are shown in parentheses; ***, ** and * indicate significance at 1%, 5% and 10% confidence levels. See Bas and Paunov (2014) for further detail.

Liberalisation efforts have also fuelled the use of mobile phones in India. Africa, like India, has experienced high growth in the number of mobile subscribers. Yet calls to Africa have not increased in the same manner as for India. International inbound traffic to India (measured by minutes or calls) was less than Africa's in 2003 but grew to 10 times higher by 2011. At the same time, the rates to call India decreased tenfold. The difference lies in whether governments let the market set the rates for incoming calls or impose a single rate through an official cartel. Between 2003 and 2011, for example, the termination charges paid by telecommunication operators carrying traffic from the United States to the rest of the world halved on a per minute basis (from around USD 0.09 to USD 0.04). For the highly competitive India market, rates dropped from more than USD 0.14 to less than USD 0.02 over the same period. In Africa on average, rates increased, suppressing demand for calls to people on that continent (OECD, 2014f).

Towards effective complementary innovation policies at the regional level

Regional development policy and innovation policy can be mutually reinforcing to promote territorial inclusiveness. Historically, regional development policy focused on simply transferring resources from wealthy to poor regions. However, a more growth-oriented approach to regional development policy has taken hold across OECD countries, spurred by the objective of strengthening the overall domestic innovation capacity, including in less developed regions (OECD, 2011b). Regional development policies can thus complement innovation policies to better support territorial inclusiveness. Furthermore, regional and local level governments themselves can take important complementary actions to improve the impact of national innovation policy instruments, such as providing innovation advisory services to firms in a nationally financed technology park.

Reaching this objective requires stronger regional capacity for innovation policy in both in OECD and non-OECD countries. The European Union has promoted the development of regional innovation strategies for many years. Most recently, it financed a platform dedicated to developing such "smart specialisation" strategies.[10] In fact, possessing a strategy is now a condition for receiving EU Structural Funds, since a significant share of those funds – particularly in the most advanced EU regions – is spent on innovation and business development. Another means of building sub-national capacity and improving the use of innovation funds is instituting a regional level council or forum for innovation. From South Africa to Denmark, such entities are used to drive greater innovation success of national policies and sub-national initiatives.[11]

6. Open questions on the economics of innovation and inclusive growth

The *All on Board – Making Inclusive Growth Happen* publication of the OECD, the result of the horizontal OECD Inclusive Growth Initiative, emphasises the critical role played by structural policies – including policies related to the labour market and competition, entrepreneurship and innovation – in achieving inclusive growth. Innovation policies can influence whether growth will result in inclusion or exclusion. By democratising innovation – i.e. empowering a wider group of innovators in society – innovation policy can serve both growth and inclusion (OECD, 2015). Conversely, selective policies – even if based on excellence – supporting innovation leaders may tend to increase inequalities, unless they go hand in hand with complementary trickle-down and diffusion policies. Hence, policy trade-offs (and complementarities) will likely arise.

The discussion above focused on the impacts of policy contexts on industrial inclusiveness, but the policies' very design might equally have impacts on industrial and territorial inclusiveness, with potential effects on social inclusiveness. Further investigation should explore whether concentrating excellence is increasingly important for growth and inclusiveness – and, conversely, whether opportunities to democratise innovation, i.e. broaden individuals and small companies' access to innovation activities and markets, support growth and inclusiveness.

Research questions to be investigated include the following:

1. What, if any, are the implications of major global trends on the industrial, territorial and social inclusiveness of innovation?
2. Is there any evidence that the concentration of rewards has changed the types of innovation and/or the pace of creative destruction? If so, do the changes occur in certain sectors and/or economic contexts?
3. What is the evidence on changing the opportunities for individuals, entrepreneurs and small companies to access innovation activities and markets? How can policy support such access opportunities, thereby democratising innovation?
4. What, if any, are the implications of policy choices aimed at supporting both growth and inclusiveness? In light of major global trends, how can innovation policies address internal imbalances in innovation capacities – including at territorial levels – while supporting growth?
5. Should policies aim to concentrate innovation capacities in order to develop excellence? Conversely, to what extent does diversifying innovation activities feature among the factors promoting growth?
6. How should policy evaluations be designed to assess the potential impacts of innovation policies on industrial, territorial and regional inclusiveness? What types of assessment methods – beyond "averages" – are desirable and feasible? Which indicators are most relevant to supporting such a policy focus?

The 2015-16 phase of the OECD Innovation for Inclusive Growth project will address the need for better diagnosis and policy development at the national and sub-national levels by analysing the policy trade-offs and complementarities of innovation and inclusiveness. The project will provide evidence on how global trends change innovation's impacts on the territorial, industrial and social dimensions of inequality. Based on the insights gained, it will complement existing policy impact assessments that focus exclusively on average policy outcomes without considering the differentiated economic and social impacts of innovation policy. Inclusiveness is typically not one of the impacts monitored in these existing assessments.

7. Conclusion

Concentration is an important feature in the organisation of innovation-related activities in developing, emerging and advanced economies. The gaps between leading innovators and laggards are substantial – particularly in emerging economies, which have some of the world's leading innovative businesses. Specialisation across sectoral activities, as well as concentration in specific regions and top research institutions, characterise most economies. The search for excellence in innovation performance drives increased concentration. The resulting lack of industrial inclusiveness may hamper opportunities for more inclusive growth dynamics. Nevertheless, a reverse trend towards a wider democratisation of innovation – whereby a large number of actors can successfully demonstrate excellence in innovation – may foster industrial inclusiveness, which in turn may have implications on social inclusiveness. Gaining a full understanding of the effect of innovation on industrial inclusiveness requires further study, notably on the impact of the current trend towards knowledge-based economies on industrial, territorial and social inclusiveness.

Notes

1. However, there were also downsides to the Green Revolution: the overuse of chemicals led to substantial land degradation (World Bank, 2006).
2. Superior innovators also have higher productivity and more substantial export capacities, and are larger than their less advanced competitors. These factors are both consequences and factors of their leading innovation performance.
3. Since firm-level input and output price data are often not available, some of the measured productivity dispersion might be due to the differential mark-ups charged by firms rather than actual differences in productivity (Foster et al., 2006).
4. Large OECD regions are those at the TL2 level – the first sub-national level. The statistic refers to 26 OECD countries with sub-national R&D data.
5. This amounts to 25.4% for employees in high-tech manufacturing sectors and 24.2% for employees in knowledge-intensive service sectors in TL2 regions (2008).
6. Small OECD regions are those at the TL3 level – the second sub-national level.
7. As (for example) Jensen (2007) or Muto and Yamano (2009) demonstrate through case studies, ICTs facilitated innovation conditions for even the smallest businesses, notably by breaking down information barriers.
8. DynEmp is an innovative project led by the OECD Directorate for Science, Technology and Innovation aiming to provide new empirical evidence on the role of creative destruction, start-ups and young firms supporting the design of better policies for employment and productivity growth, based on confidential firm level data from national business registers.
9. In cross-licensing arrangements, IP owners grant each other licences to exploit IP rights for part or all of their IP portfolios.
10. See http://s3platform.jrc.ec.europa.eu/ for further details.
11. South Africa's Department of Science and Technology has promoted the concept of a Regional Innovation Forum bringing together public and private actors to support the economic and social development of the country's various regions through innovation. The forums are progressively being launched in provinces throughout the country. In Denmark, Regional Growth Forums in each region help guide their economic development, growth and innovation strategies. These public-private forums have 20 members: regional and municipal public officials, 6 business people, representatives from the higher education and research communities, and trade union representatives. They meet four to six times per year depending on the region. The presidents of the Regional Growth Forums are also members of the Danish Growth Council.

References

Acs, Z.J., D.B. Audretsch and M.P. Feldman (1994), "R&D spillovers and recipient firm size", *The Review of Economics and Statistics*, Vol. 76/2, pp. 336-40.

Agrawal, A. and A. Goldfarb (2008), "Restructuring Research: Communication Costs and the Democratization of University Innovation", *American Economic Review*, Vol. 98/4, pp. 1578-1590.

Alfaro, L., A. Charlton and F. Kanczuk (2009), "Plant-Size Distribution and Cross-Country Income Differences", in *NBER International Seminar on Macroeconomics*, NBER, Cambridge.

Arthur, W.B. (2007), "The structure of invention", *Research Policy*, Vol. 36/2, pp. 274-287.

Audretsch, D. and M. Feldman (2004), "Knowledge Spillovers and the Geography of Innovation", in *Handbook of Regional and Urban Economics*, Vol. 4, North Holland Publishing, Amsterdam.

Audretsch, D. and M. Feldman (1996), "R&D spillovers and the geography of innovation and production", *The American Economic Review*, pp. 630-640.

Bas, M. and C. Paunov (2014), "The unequal effect of India's industrial liberalization on firms' decision to innovate: Do business conditions matter?", OECD, unpublished manuscript.

Bloom, N., M. Schankerman and J. Van Reenen (2013), "Identifying Technology Spillovers and Product Market Rivalry", *Econometrica*, Vol. 81(4), pp. 1347-1393.

Combes P.-P., G. Duranton and L. Gobillon (2011), "The Identification of Agglomeration Economies", *Journal of Economic Geography*, Vol. 11/2, pp. 253-266.

Crescenzi, R., A. Rodríguez-Pose and M. Storper (2012), "The territorial dynamics of innovation in China and India", *Journal of Economic Geography*, Vol. 12, pp. 1055-1085.

David, P.A., S.R. Johansson and A. Pozzi (2010), "The Demography Of An Early Mortality Transition: Life Expectancy, Survival And Mortality Rates For Britain's Royals, 500-1799," *Discussion Papers in Economic and Social History*, Vol. 83, University of Oxford, Oxford.

Ding, W.W. et al. (2010), "The impact of information technology on academic scientists' productivity and collaboration patterns", *Management Science*, Vol. 56/9, pp. 1439-1461.

Donner, J. (2006), "The use of mobile phones by microentrepreneurs in Kigali, Rwanda: Changes to social and business networks", *Information Technologies and International Development*, Vol. 3, pp. 3-19.

Donner, J. (2004), "Microentrepreneurs and Mobiles: An Exploration of the Uses of Mobile Phones by Small Business Owners in Rwanda", *Information Technologies and International Development* 2, pp. 1-21.

Duncombe, R. and R. Heeks (2002), "Enterprise across the digital divide: Information systems and rural microenterprise in Botswana", *Journal of International Development*, Vol. 14, pp. 61-74.

Esselaar, S. et al. (2007), "ICT usage and its impact on profitability of SMEs in 13 African Countries", *Information Technologies and International Development*, Vol. 4, pp. 87-100.

European Commission, *2013 EU Industrial R&D Investment Scoreboard*, Publications Office of the European Union, Luxembourg.

Fernandes, A. and C. Paunov (forthcoming), "The Risks of Innovation: Are Innovating Firms Less Likely to Die?", *The Review of Economics and Statistics*, forthcoming.

Foster, L., J. Haltiwanger and C.J. Krizan (2006), "Market selection, reallocation, and restructuring in the US retail trade sector in the 1990s", *The Review of Economics and Statistics*, Vol. 88(4), pp. 748-758.

Görg, H. and D. Greenaway (2004), "Much ado about nothing? Do domestic firms really benefit from foreign direct investment?", *The World Bank Research Observer*, Vol. 19(2), pp. 171-197.

Gupta, R., S. Sankhe, R. Dobbs, J. Woetzel, A. Madgavkar and A. Hasyagar (2014), *From poverty to empowerment: India's imperative for jobs, growth, and effective basic services*, McKinsey Global Institute, McKinsey & Company, New York.

Harris, B. (2004), "Public health, nutrition and the decline of mortality: The McKeown thesis revisited", *Social History of Medicine*, Vol. 17(3), pp. 379-427.

Helsley, R.W. and W.C. Strange (1990), "Matching and agglomeration economies in a system of cities", *Regional Science and Urban Economics*, Vol. 20(2), pp. 189-212

Hollingsworth, T. (1957), "A Demographic Study of the British Ducal Families", *Population Studies*, Vol. 11, pp. 4-26.

Hsieh C.-T. and P. Klenow (2009), "Misallocation and Manufacturing TFP in China and India", *Quarterly Journal of Economics*, Vol. 124, pp. 1403-1448.

Hsieh, C.-T. and B.A. Olken (2014), "The Missing "Missing Middle'", *Journal of Economic Perspectives*, American Economic Association, Vol. 28(3), pp. 89-108, summer.

Hu, A.G., G.H. Jefferson and Q. Jinchang (2005), R&D and technology transfer: Firm-level evidence from Chinese industry, *Review of Economics and Statistics*, 87(4), pp. 780-786.

Human Mortality Database, University of California, Berkeley, and Max Planck Institute for Demographic Research (Germany), available at www.mortality.org (data downloaded in January 2014).

InnoCentive (2014), InnoCentive website, www.innocentive.com (accessed on 1 December 2014).

Jaffe, A.B., M. Trajtenberg and R. Henderson (1993), "Geographic knowledge spillovers as evidenced by patent citations", *Quarterly Journal of Economics*, 108(3), pp. 577-598.

Jensen, R. (2007), "The Digital Provide: Information (Technology), Market Performance, and Welfare in the South Indian Fisheries Sector", *The Quarterly Journal of Economics*, Vol. 122, pp. 879-924.

Johansson, S.R. (2010), "Medics, Monarchs and Mortality, 1600-1800: Origins of the Knowledge-Driven Health Transition in Europe", *Discussion Papers in Economic and Social History*, Vol. 85, University of Oxford, Oxford.

Keller, W. (2004), "International Technology Diffusion", *Journal of Economic Literature*, Vol. 42, pp. 752-782.

Kokko, A., R. Tansini and M.C. Zejan (1996), "Local technological capability and productivity spillovers from FDI in the Uruguayan manufacturing sector", *The Journal of Development Studies*, Vol. 32(4), pp. 602-611.

Krugman, P. (1991), "Increasing Returns and Economic Geography", *The Journal of Political Economy*, Vol. 99(3), pp. 483-499.

Lanjouw, J. and M. Schankerman (2004), "Protecting intellectual property rights: Are small firms handicapped?", *The Journal of Law and Economics*, Vol. 47(1), pp. 45-74.

Lee, K. (2014), "Innovation and Upgrading for Inclusive Growth: Implications for LICs/MICs", presentation given at the Growth Dialogue Forum in Malaysia.

Lembcke, A., R. Ahrend and K. Maguire (2015), "Spatial Aspects of Inclusive Growth: The Distribution of Regional Benefits from Innovation", *OECD Regional Development Working Papers*, forthcoming.

Marinescu, I. and R. Rathelo (2014), "The Geography of Job Search and Mismatch Unemployment", unpublished manuscript.

Muto, M. and T. Yamano (2009), "The impact of mobile phone coverage expansion on market participation: Panel data evidence from Uganda", *World Development*, Vol. 37(12), pp. 1887-1896.

New York Times (2013), "Yahoo Orders Home Workers Back to the Office", *New York Times*, 25 February 2013, www.nytimes.com/2013/02/26/technology/yahoo-orders-home-workers-back-to-the-office.html (accessed on 15 July 2014).

OECD (2015), *All on Board, Making Inclusive Growth Happen*, OECD Publishing, Paris, http://dx.doi.org/10.1787/9789264218512-en.

OECD (2014a), *OECD Economic Surveys: Germany*, OECD Publishing, Paris, http://dx.doi.org/10.1787/eco_surveys-deu-2014-en.

OECD (2014b), *National Intellectual Property Systems, Innovation and Economic Development: With perspectives on Colombia and Indonesia*, OECD Publishing, Paris, http://dx.doi.org: 10.1787/9789264204485-en.

OECD (2014d), "The Role of Data in Promoting Growth and Well-Being", webpage, www.oecd.org/sti/ieconomy/data-driven-innovation.htm.

OECD (2014e), Time to terminate termination charges?, *OECD Insights*, 13 June 2014, http://oecd insights.org/2014/06/13/time-to-terminate-termination-charges/.

OECD (2014f), "International Cables, Gateways, Backhaul and International Exchange Points", *OECD Digital Economy Papers*, No. 232, OECD Publishing, http://dx.doi.org/10.1787/5jz8m9jf3wkl-en.

OECD (2013a), *Crisis Squeezes Income and Puts Pressure on Inequality and Poverty*, OECD Publishing, Paris.

OECD (2013b), *OECD Regional Statistics* (database), OECD, http://dx.doi.org/10.1787/region-data-en.

OECD (2013c), *OECD Science, Technology and Industry Scoreboard 2013*, OECD Publishing, Paris, http://dx.doi.org/10.1787/sti_scoreboard-2013-en.

OECD (2013d), *OECD Regions at a Glance 2013*, OECD Publishing, Paris, http://dx.doi.org/10.1787/reg_glance-2013-en.

OECD (2013e), *The Internet Economy on the Rise: Progress since the Seoul Declaration*, OECD Publishing, http://dx.doi.org/10.1787/9789264201545-en.

OECD (2011a), *Divided We Stand: Why Inequality Keep Rising*, OECD Publishing, Paris, http://dx.doi.org/10.1787/9789264119536-en.

OECD (2011b), *Regions and Innovation Policy*, OECD Publishing, Paris, http://dx.doi.org/10.1787/9789264097803-en.

OECD (2010), *ICTs for Development: Improving Policy Coherence*, The Development Dimension, OECD Publishing, Paris, http://dx.doi.org/10.1787/9789264077409-en.

OECD (2009a), *OECD Patent Statistics Manual*, OECD Publishing, Paris, http://dx.doi.org/10.1787/9789264056442-en.

OECD (2009b), *Internet Access for Development*, The Development Dimension, OECD Publishing, Paris, *http://dx.doi.org/10.1787/9789264056312-en*.

OECD/Eurostat (2005), *Oslo Manual: Guidelines for Collecting and Interpreting Innovation Data, 3rd Edition*, The Measurement of Scientific and Technological Activities, OECD Publishing, Paris, *http://dx.doi.org/10.1787/9789264013100-en*.

Paunov, C. (2014), "Democratizing Intellectual Property Systems: How Corruption Hinders Equal Opportunities for Firms", unpublished manuscript.

Paunov, C. (2013), "Innovation and Inclusive Development: A Discussion of the Main Policy Issues", *OECD Science, Technology and Industry Working Paper* (No. 2013/1), OECD Publishing.

Paunov, C. and D. Guellec (2015), "Innovation and Inclusive Growth", unpublished manuscript.

Paunov, C. and V. Rollo (2014), "Has the Internet Fostered Inclusive Innovation in the Developing World?", unpublished manuscript.

Radjou, N., J. Prabhu and S. Ahuja (2013), *L'Innovation jugaad. Redevenons ingénieux!*, Éditions Diateino, Paris.

Salmi, J. (2013), "The race for excellence – A marathon not a sprint", *University World News* 254, 13 January, *www.universityworldnews.com/article.php?story=20130108161422529* (accessed on 7 March 2013).

Stiglitz, J.E., A. Sen and J.-P. Fitoussi (2009), *Report of the Commission on Measurement of Economic Performance and Social Progress*, *www.stiglitz-sen-titoussi.fr/en/index.htm*.

Syverson, C. (2004), "Product Substitutability and Productivity Dispersion", *Review of Economics and Statistics*, MIT Press Journals, Cambridge, MA.

The Economist (2014), "Special report: Tech startups", 18 January 2014, *The Economist*, London.

Von Hippel, E. (2005), *Democratizing Innovation*, MIT Press Journals, Cambridge, MA.

World Bank (2014a), *Poverty and Inequality Database*, *http://databank.worldbank.org/data/views/variableselection/selectvariables.aspx?source=Poverty-and-Inequality-Database* (accessed in May 2014)

World Bank (2014b), *World Development Indicators* (database), *http://data.worldbank.org/data-catalog/world-development-indicators* (accessed in May 2014).

World Bank (2006), *Enhancing Agricultural Innovation. How to Go Beyond the Strengthening of Research Systems*, World Bank, Washington, DC.

ORGANISATION FOR ECONOMIC CO-OPERATION AND DEVELOPMENT

The OECD is a unique forum where governments work together to address the economic, social and environmental challenges of globalisation. The OECD is also at the forefront of efforts to understand and to help governments respond to new developments and concerns, such as corporate governance, the information economy and the challenges of an ageing population. The Organisation provides a setting where governments can compare policy experiences, seek answers to common problems, identify good practice and work to co-ordinate domestic and international policies.

The OECD member countries are: Australia, Austria, Belgium, Canada, Chile, the Czech Republic, Denmark, Estonia, Finland, France, Germany, Greece, Hungary, Iceland, Ireland, Israel, Italy, Japan, Korea, Luxembourg, Mexico, the Netherlands, New Zealand, Norway, Poland, Portugal, the Slovak Republic, Slovenia, Spain, Sweden, Switzerland, Turkey, the United Kingdom and the United States. The European Commission takes part in the work of the OECD.

OECD Publishing disseminates widely the results of the Organisation's statistics gathering and research on economic, social and environmental issues, as well as the conventions, guidelines and standards agreed by its members.